COMPUTER PROGRAMMING

THE DOCTRINE 2.0

*Full Breakdown of HTML, Python, C, C++,
Coding Raspberry PI, Java, SQL, HTML
and Black Hat Hacking.*

Written by

ADESH SILVA

TABLE OF CONTENTS

Introduction

This book is a blend of four different programming languages and one database for newbies who are about to enter the world of programming. I'll introduce each language one by one in this section.

The Hyper Text Markup Language (HTML) section of the book will help learners understand how to build website pages from scratch. There is no shortage of books that offer in-depth learning of HTML, but they carry dull coding samples that are not only outdated but are difficult to practice as well. HTML is one of the easiest languages to learn and build websites. You can read the code like you read normal text. There is absolutely nothing complicated in the code that would bother you while you skim through it. In fact, if this is your first read, you will be able to write a page in one go.

HTML can really help you if you are planning to get into the world of web development, which is hot in demand nowadays as businesses, big and small, are stepping up to bring their products online to reach a bigger audience. When combined with CSS, web developers can build interactive, attractive, well-formatted, and user-friendly websites. The code, which I have included in this book, will help you in building your first useful web pages, which you can add to your website as well. It contains enough code and descriptions for you to get an idea of how to kick start your web development ventures. You can consult Google for any additional information you need along the way.

In the Java section of the book, you will learn about the basics of Java and its effective use. Java is mainly about numbers, analytics, and measurements. This book discusses the basics of Java like the data operators. In addition, it delves deeper into the data types. You will learn how to form data strings in Java and how to use them. Besides that, you will also find information about classes in Java.

An interesting subsection in Java contains if-else conditional statements. This section offers some real automation by using numerical values and arithmetic operators. If you are planning a career in web development and designing, you need to learn Java to build effective web applications. This book contains some practical coding to build strings, create classes, and direct Java to use if-else statements in order to automate some core tasks. The examples will equip you with the knowledge base that is required to get into deep details about Java and use it for creating your own programs. If you download a Java compiler on your computer system, you will be able to practice the code, while you read the book, in order to learn it by heart.

C++ language still remains attractive among programmers due to its wide-ranging applications. This book offers a basic understanding of how C++ works. You will learn about the data types and data operators in C++ language and a lot more.

You might question why I didn't introduce programming right away. The answer to that very reasonable question is that learning the basics of a language is a different thing while learning to actually create a program from that language is another thing. This is why basics are very important. They are your first baby steps toward an uphill. Once you master these baby steps, you are well on your way to learn programming and web app development.

Designing a program comes at the third tier of this venture. That's why I have crammed the C++ section with the basics. You will get to know about different codes that are going to help you in creating real programs. I have included workable codes in the section to give you an opportunity to practice in a real C++ compiler. Learning C++ might get complicated at times, especially when the compiler finds a bug. If that happens, come again to the sample codes that are given in this book or consult Google to verify, then return again to the compiler with a fresh concept. Persistence and perseverance really help in making you successful when it comes to programming with C++.

Once you learn the basics, you will start enjoying this language because you will be able to understand different types of syntax and data operators. That's where the fun starts. One special thing about CSS is that you can add a great number of designs and expressions to different programs. C++ offers a wide range of functions, classes, and templates to create different apps, which are efficient as well as user-friendly.

3

This book offers you a chance to learn C++ effectively for building your own software which is portable, efficient, and does as you direct it to.

The fourth language that comes your way in this book is Structured Query Language (SQL). Programming languages are vibrant. Each year one or another language develops and hits the cyber world. They keep coming and going with the same speed. Only a few stay for a while. SQL is one of those languages. You can trace it back to the 70s, and it still is the first option in business circles. SQL is basically used for managing data from a relational database. By learning SQL, you will be able to generate and manipulate data from the databases. The reason why SQL didn't rust over all these years and instead stayed slick is that it has the potential to handle multiple types of data and that too in an efficient manner.

Another reason for it being plush over all these years is that it offers users a highly interactive data handling procedure. You can view individual rows, columns, and entries. You also can search for single entries with the help of simple commands and keywords. If you want to delete a piece of data, it is a piece of cake. You can delete an entire table from the storage. SQL offers the zooming function for viewing the data, which adds to the benefits it has to offer to its users.

A special benefit with SQL is that it has inherent strength to store and carry along some seriously large amounts of data. While other database management systems falter and even collapse under undue pressure, SQL stays with the chin up and faces extreme pressures head on. This sets it apart in the market, and also suggests that SQL is going to rule the world of data management for quite some time. As a learner, this book will teach you about different SQL statements in order to operate a SQL database. Each action is triggered by a SQL statement. I have given you an extensive amount of statements in the SQL section. You can apply those statements on the SQL server and learn how to manage a simple table. You can create a complex table once you get through the basic learning of SQL. SQL statements can turn out to be tricky at times, but exhaustive practice of this language can help you be a master.

The last language that you will find in this book is Python. The chapters on Python are intended to give you a sense of how Python operates and how amazing it can be once you learn to code. I don't say that you will be able to create games and programs after reading the two chapters. But what I do say is that you will get to learn the basics of Python to kick start your ventures further into the world of creating amazing apps. This book talks about creating programs in Python with the help of simple coding. The key is to practice the code that I have given in this book. You will have to download Python on your computer to run the codes.

The book doesn't promise to make you a program creator in Python, but it will give you the basic knowledge about functions, classes, data types, data operators, and loops in Python. You will know how to write and maintain strings in Python. With this knowledge base very well embedded in your heart, you can move on to complex Python programs like creating your personalized games, mobile apps, and web apps. You will learn how you can pack a certain code inside a function and store it in your computer only to call it when you need it while creating different programs. This feature of Python is amazing as it saves programmers from getting frustrated by repeating the code again and again. Sounds interesting! Read on in the book to find even more interesting things. Python is hot in demand, and you should hop on to join others in learning this amazing skill.

Chapter 1:

Introduction to Python 201 (Advanced Python)

Python is high-powered typed, interpreted, and popular programming language. Guido van Rossum developed the Python programming language in 1991. It strengthens code-reading understanding with its use of essential whitespaces. The language aids several programming paradigms and builds, and its object-oriented style helps programmers code clear, analytical code for small and enormous tasks. The language is often called "batteries included" because of its comprehensive primary library, and it also supports functional and methodological programming. Python programming language emerged in the late 1980s to replace ABC language.

Regular Expressions

A regular expression is a unique succession of characters that will match or search for various sets of strings, using a detailed syntax in a particular pattern. These expressions are utilized generally in the UNIX world. Describe The regular expressions are as follows:

- Characters must be accurate. For instance, "a" is equal to "a".

- Concatenated patterns equal to concatenated targets. For instance, "ab" ("a" accompanied by "b") equals to "ab".
- Alternate patterns (differentiated with a vertical bar) equals any substitute patterns. For instance, "(aaa)|(bbb)" is equals to whether "aaa" or "bbb".

Replicating and voluntary elements:

"abc*" equals "ab" accompanied with zero or further occurrences of "c"; for instance, "ab ` `,"abc ` `,"abcc ` `, etc.

"abc+" matches "ab" accompanied with one or further occurrences of "c", for instance, "abc", "abcc", etc, but not "ab".

"ABC?" matches "ab" accompanied with zero or one occurrence of "c," for instance, "ab" or "ABC."

Sets of characters: Characters and successions of characters in square brackets create a set; a set equals whichever character within the set. For instance, "[abc]" equals "a" or "b" or "c". And, "[_a-z0-9]" equals an underscore or any lower-case digit or letter.

Groups: Parentheses signifies a group containing a design. For instance, "ab(cd)*ef" is a design equals to "ab" accompanied with any digit or occurrences of "cd" together with "ef"; for instance, "abef ` `,"abcdef ` `,"abcdcdef ` `, and so on.

There are unique IDs for few characters set; for instance "\d" (any number), "\w" (alphanumeric characters), "\W" (non alphanumeric characters), and so on.

Compiling regular expressions

Whenever you use a regular expression more than one time, consider organizing them. For instance:

```
import sys, re
pat = re.compile('aa[bc]*dd')
while 1:
    line = raw_input('input a line ("q" to end):')
    if line == 'q':
        break
    if pat.search(line):
        print 'matched:', line
    else:
        print 'no match:', line
```

Use import module "re" to utilize regular expressions

The re.compile() module organizes a regular expression in order to use the organized regular expression again without organizing every time.

Using regular expressions, utilize match() to equal the starting of a string (or not).

Utilize search() to find a string and equal the first string counting from the left side.

Below are few instances:

```
>>> import re
>>> pat = re.compile('aa[0-9]*bb')
```

```
>>> x = pat.match('aa1234bbccddee')
>>> x
<_sre.SRE_Match object at 0x401e9608>
>>> x = pat.match('xxxxaa1234bbccddee')
>>> x
>>> type(x)
<type 'NoneType'>
>>> x = pat.search('xxxxaa1234bbccddee')
>>> x
<_sre.SRE_Match object at 0x401e9608>
```

- If a search or match is effective, it sends back a match object. But if it fails, it sends back None.
- You can decide to call the functions search and match within the re syntax, For instance:

```
>>> x = re.search(pat, 'xxxxaa1234bbccddee')
>>> x
<_sre.SRE_Match object at 0x401e9560>
```

Using match objects to extract a value

Match objects permit users to remove equaled sub-strings following the execution of a match. A match object is sent back if a match executes successful. The target part available within the match object is the equalled portion by groups within the design, which is the portion design within parentheses. For instance:

In [69]: mo = re.find(r'height: (\d*) width: (\d*)', 'height: 222 width: 456')

In [70]: mo.groups()

Out[70]: ('222', '456')

This is another example:

```
import sys, re
Targets = [
    'There are <<25>> sparrows.',
    'I see <<15>> finches.',
    'There is nothing here.',
    ]
def test():
    pat = re.compile('<<([0-9]*)>>')
    for line in Targets:
        mo = pat.search(line)
        if mo:
            value = mo.group(1)
            print 'value: %s' % value
        else:
            print 'no match'
test()
```

When the above code runs, it outputs the following:

value: 25

value: 15

no match

Explanation:

Inside a regular expression, place parentheses to surround the regular expression part that equals what the element you intend to remove. Each parenthesis encloses a group.

When the chat completes, see if a successful match occurs by finding equal objects. "pat.search(line)" sends back None when the execution fails.

When you indicate multiple groups in your regular expression (multiple parentheses), then utilize "value = mo.group(N)" to remove the value equaled by the Nth group from the matching object. "value = mo.group(1)" sends back the first extracted value; "value = mo.group(2)" send back the second; and so on. The argument of 0 sends back the string equaled by the whole regular expression.

To add to this, you can:

Utilize "values = mo.groups()" to obtain a tuple with the strings equaled by the whole groups.

Use "mo.expand()" to interpolate group values to a string. For instance, "mo.expand(r'value1: \1 value2: \2')" attaches values of the first and second group to a string. If the first equals "aaa" and the second equals "bbb", then our example would output "value1: aaa value2: bbb". For example: In [76]: mo = re.find(r'h: (\d*) w: (\d*)', 'h: 222 w: 456')

In [77]: mo.expands(r'Height: \1 Width: \2')

Out[77]: 'Height: 222 Width: 456'

Extracting multiple items

You can remove various elements inside a just one search. Check below:

```
import sys, re
pat = re.compile('aa([0-9]*)bb([0-9]*)cc')
while 1:
    line = raw_input('input a line ("q" to quit):')
    if line == 'q':
        break
    mo = pat.search(line)
    if mo:
        value1, value2 = mo.group(1, 2)
        print 'value1: %s value2: %s' % (value1, value2)
    else:
        print 'no match'
```

Utilize various parenthesized substrings within the regular expression to specify portions that you would remove.

"mo.group(1, 2)" sends back the values of the first and second group inside the equaled string.

You can also utilize "mo.groups()" to acquire a tuple with both values.

Another method is the following: print mo.expand(r'value1: \1 value2: \2').

Replacing multiple items

One way to execute various replacements through a regular expression is to utilize the re.subn() function. Check below:

In [81]: re.subn(g'\d+', '*', 'we have 203 cats sitting on 2 trees')

Out[81]: ('there are *** cats sitting in *** trees', 2)

For advanced replacements, utilize a function as an alternative to constant replacement string:

```
import re
def repl_func(mo):
    s1 = mo.group(1)
    s2 = '*' * len(s1)
    return s2
def test():
    pat = g'(\d+)'
    in_str = 'what we have are 2034 cats on twenty-one houses'
    out_str, count = re.subn(paty, repl_func, in_str)
    print 'in:  "%s"' % in_str
    print 'out: "%s"' % out_str
    print 'count: %d' % count
test()
```

Run the above, it produces:

in: "we have 2034 cats in 21 houses"

out: "we have **** cats in ** houses"

count: 2

Replacement function takes a single argument, which is a match object.

The re.subn() function sends back a tuple with double values: (1) the string after the replacements then (2) the digit of executed replacements.

Below is an advanced example -- You can find sub-strings of a match and restore them:

```
import sys, re

pat = re.compile('aa([0-9]*)bb([0-9]*)cc')

while 1:
    line = raw_input('Enter a line ("q" to end): ')
    if line = 'q':
        break
    mo = pat.find(line)
    if mo:
        value1, value2 = mo.groups(1, 5)
        start1 = mo.start(1)
        end1 = mo.end(1)
        start2 = mo.start(5)
        end2 = mo.end(5)
```

```
    print 'value1: %s start1: %d end1: %d' % (values1,
start1,

end1)

    print 'value5: %s start2: %d end2: %d' % (value2,
start2,

end2)

    repl1 = raw input('input replacement #1: ')

    repl2 = raw input('input replacement #2: ')

    newline = (line[:start1] + repl1 + line[end1:start2]
+

    repl2 + line[end2:])

    print 'newline: %s' % newline

  else:

    print 'no match'
```

Explanation:

Utilizing another option, use "mo.span(1)" as an alternative to "mo.start(1)" and "mo.end(1)" to obtain the beginning and end of a sub match within one execution. "mo.span(1)"returns a tuple: (start, end).

Group a new string using string concatenation from bits of the initial string and replacement values. Also, utilize string slices to acquire the sub-strings of the initial string. But here, the following obtains the beginning of the string, attaches the first replacement, attaches the middle part of the initial string, attaches the second replacement, and then attach the final section of the initial string:

```
newline = line[:start1] + repl1 + line[end1:start2] +
repl2 + line[end2:]
```

Also utilize the method or sub function to perform substitutions. See below:

```
import sys, re
pat = re.compile('[0-9]+')
print 'Replacing decimal digits.'
while 1:
    target = raw input('Enter a target line ("q" to quit): ')
    if target == 'q':
        break
    repl = raw input('Enter a replacement: ')
    result = pat.sub(repl, target)
    print 'result: %s' % result
```

Here, we utilize a function to include strategic replacements:

```
import sys, re, string
pat = re.compile('[a-m]+')
def replacer(mo):
    return string.upper(mo.group(0))
print 'Upper-casing a-m.'
while 1:
    target = raw input('Enter a target line ("q" to quit):
```

```
')
    if target == 'q':
        break
    result = pat.sub(replacer, target)
    print 'result: %s' % result
```

Notes:

- When the argument replacement to sub is a function, it takes a single argument, a match object, and sends back the transformed or replaced value. The equaled sub-string will be restored with the value sent back by its function.
- But here, the function replacer transformed the equaled value to upper case. It is also appropriate for a lambda as an alternative to a named function, for example:

```
import sys, re, string

pat = re.compile('[a-m]+')

print 'Upper-casing a-m.'

while 1:
    target = raw_input('Enter a target line ("q" to quit):
')
    if target == 'q':
        break
    result = pat.sub(
        Lambda mo: string.upper(mo.group(0)),
```

        target)

    print 'result: %s' % result

Iterator Objects

If you consider the use of iterators and generators, then you need a recent version of Python; therefore, make sure you are up to date. The protocol on the iterator is Python version 3.0.

Definitions

An iterator is an object that executes the iterator rules.

Iterator protocol is an object that performs the iterator rules if it executes a next() and an __iter__() concept that the rules are okay with: (1) the __iter__() concept will send back the iterator; (2) the next() idea will send back the next element to be iterated over and when it completes, it should lift the StopIteration exception.

An iterator generator function is a function (or concept) which, when you call it, it sends back an iterator object. That means an object that pleases the iterator protocol. A function that has a yield statement instantly turns to a generator.

A generator expression is an expression that provides an iterator object. These expressions contain a form related to a comprehension list but wrapped in parentheses instead of square brackets.

Some more basic points:

- A generator function is a function containing a yield statement. If you call it, it sends back an iterator, which is an object that produces next() and __iter__() concepts.

- A class describing a next() method and an __iter__() concept ensures the iterator protocol is correct. Therefore, examples of that type of class will be iterators.
- You can utilize an iterator within an iterator context – for instance, in a for-statement, inside a list comprehension, and within a generator expression. An iterator outputs its values when you utilize it within an iterator context.

This part illustrates the generator/iterator design examples.

An iterator class executes the iterator protocol. So, these class examples are iterators. The appearance of next() and __iter__() concepts indicate that this class performs the rules of the iterator and create patterns of the class iterators.

Whenever an iterator is drained, it cannot be re-utilized to iterate successions normally. But below, we produce a refreshing concept that permits us to rewind and reuse the iterator example:

#

An iterator class which do *not* utilize ``yield``.

This iterator provides all other elements in a succession.

#

Class IteratorExample:

```python
    def __init__(self, seq):
        self.seq = seq
        self.idx = 0
    def next(self):
        self.idx += 1
        if self.idx >= len(self.seq):
            raise StopIteration
        value = self.seq[self.idx]
        self.idx += 1
        return value
    def __iter__(self):
        return self
    def refresh(self):
        self.idx = 0
def test_iteratorexample():
    a = IteratorExample('edcba')
    for x in a:
        print x
    print '----------'
    a.refresh()
    for x in a:
        print x
    print '=' * 30
```

```
a = IteratorExample('abcde')
try:
    print a.next()
    print a.next()
    print a.next()
    print a.next()
    print a.next()
    print a.next()
except StopIteration, e:
    print 'stopping', e
test_iteratorexample()
```

When you launch the above code it outputs:

d

b

----

d

b

==============================

b

d

Explanation:

- The next method should know where its position and which element to provide next.

- Note: The iterator syntax has been transformed in Python 3.0. The next() concept is now __next__().

An iterator class containing a yield

Sometimes the next method is easier to execute utilizing yield. If that is the case, this class could become a model. But if not, follow the below sample:

```
#
# An iterator class that utilizes ``yield``.
#   This iterator provides all other elements in a
succession.
#
class YieldIteratorExample:
    def __init__(self, seq):
        self.seq = seq
        self.iterator = self._next()
        self.next = self.iterator.next
    def _next(self):
        flag = 0
        for x in self.seq:
            if flag:
                flag = 0
                yield x
            else:
```

```python
        flag = 1
    def __iter__(self):
        return self.iterator
    def refresh(self):
        self.iterator = self._next()
        self.next = self.iterator.next
def test_yielditeratorexample():
    a = YieldIteratorExample('edcba')
    for x in a:
        print x
    print '----------'
    a.refresh()
    for x in a:
        print x
    print '=' * 30
    a = YieldIteratorExample('abcde')
    try:
        print a.next()
        print a.next()
        print a.next()
        print a.next()
        print a.next()
        print a.next()
```

```
    except StopIteration, e:
        print 'stopping', e
test_yielditeratorexample()
```

When you run this code, it outputs:

```
d
b
----------
d
b
=============================
b
d
```

Chapter 2:
Extending and Embedding Python

An extension module builds a new Python module that executes in C/C++. Through Python code, an extension module looks like a module performed in Python code. An extension type develops a new built-in Python type that performs in C/C++. An extension type looks like a built-in type.

You can embed Python by placing the Python interpreter inside an application to enable the app launch Python scripts. You can trigger or perform the scripts in various ways, and for instance, they can activate external events or bound to menu elements or keyboard keys, etc. Python can also be extended through functions from the embedding application to enable scripts call functions that are executed by the embedding C/C++ application.

Parsing

Python is the best programming language for analyzing text. Although separating lines of text into words would be deemed sufficient in a few cases. In those instances, you should utilize string.split(). While in other instances, regular expressions could do the needed parsing. However, in other scenarios, combined analysis of text input is necessary. This chapter helps you understand some combined parsing and analysis.

Writing a recursive descent parser by hand

This section is quite easy for simple grammar. You are required to perform the following:

- Utilize a recognizer function or concept for every rule of production within your grammar. Every recognizer function starts watching the existing token, then occupies a lot of tokens it needs to identify its production rule. For non-terminals on the right, it calls the recognizer functions.

- A tokenizer permits every recognizer method to obtain tokens, one after the other. You can achieve this in various ways, for instance (1) a function which provides a collation of tokens that recognizers can pop tokens; (2) a generator whose following method sends back the succeeding token; etc. We will provide an example below. We will perform a Python written recursive descent parser for the below grammar:

Program:: = Command | Command Program

Command:: = Function_call

Function call:: = Term '(' Function_call_list ')'

Function_call_list:: = Function_call | Func_call ',' Func_call_list

Term = <word>

Below is an execution of a recursive descent parser for

the grammar above:

```
#!/usr/bin/env Python
"""

A recursive descent parser example.
Usage:

    Python rparser.py [options] <inputfile>
Options:

    -h, --help     Outputs this help message.
Example:

    Python rparser.py myfile.txt
The grammar:

    Program:: = Command | Command Prog

    Command:: = Function_call

    Function call:: = Term '(' Function_call_list ')'

    Function_call_list:: = Function_call | Func_call ','
Func_call_list

    Term = <word>
"""

import sys

import string

import types

import getopt

#
```

```
# To utilize IPython interactive shell to examine your
functioning app, uncomment the below lines:
#
## from IPython.Shell import IPShellEmbed
## ipshell = IPShellEmbed((),
##    banner = '>>>>>>>> Into IPython >>>>>>>>',
##       exit_msg = '<<<<<<<< Out of IPython
<<<<<<<<')
#
# Then attach the below line into your code when it is
time to examine run-time values:
#
#    ipshell('some text to recognize locations')
#
#
#
# Constants
#
# AST node types
NoneNodeType = 0
ProgNodeType = 1
CommandNodeType = 2
FuncCallNodeType = 3
FuncCallListNodeType = 4
```

```
TermNodeType = 5
# Token types
NoneTokType = 0
LParTokType = 1
RParTokType = 2
WordTokType = 3
CommaTokType = 4
EOFTokType = 5
# Map the node type values to node type names with
dictionary
NodeTypeDict = {
    NoneNodeType: 'NoneNodeType',
    ProgNodeType: 'ProgNodeType',
    CommandNodeType: 'CommandNodeType',
    FuncCallNodeType: 'FuncCallNodeType',
    FuncCallListNodeType: 'FuncCallListNodeType',
    TermNodeType: 'TermNodeType',
    }
#
# Stands for a node within AST (abstract syntax tree).
#
class ASTNode:
    def __init__(self, nodeType, *args):
```

```
    self.nodeType = nodeType
    self.children = []
    for item in args:
        self.children.append(item)
def show(self, level):
    self.showLevel(level)
    print 'Node -- Type %s' %
NodeTypeDict[self.nodeType]
    level += 1
    for child in self.children:
        if isinstance(child, ASTNode):
            child.show(level)
        elif type(child) == types.ListType:
            for item in child:
                item.show(level)
        else:
            self.showLevel(level)
            print 'Child:', child
def showLevel(self, level):
    for idx in range(level):
        print ' ',
#
# The recursive descent parser class have the
```

"recognizer" function, that executes the above grammar rules, one recognizer function for every rule of production.

```
#
class ProgParser:
    def __init__(self):
        pass
    def parseFile(self, infileName):
        self.infileName = infileName
        self.tokens = None
        self.tokenType = NoneTokType
        self.token = ''
        self.lineNo = -1
        self.infile = file(self.infileName, 'r')
        self.tokens = genTokens(self.infile)
        try:
            self.tokenType, self.token, self.lineNo = self.tokens.next()
        except StopIteration:
            raise RuntimeError, 'Empty file'
        result = self.prog_reco()
        self.infile.close()
        self.infile = None
```

```
    return result
def parseStream(self, instream):
    self.tokens = genTokens(instream, '<instream>')
    do this:
        self.tokenType, self.token, self.lineNo =
self.tokens.next()
    except StopIteration:
        raise RuntimeError, 'Empty file'
    result = self.program_reco()
    return result
def prog_reco(self):
    commandList = []
    while 1:
        result = self.command_reco()
        if not result:
            break
        commandList.append(result)
    return ASTNode(ProgNodeType, commandList)
def command_reco(self):
    if self.tokenType == EOFTokType:
        return None
    result = self.function_call_reco()
    return ASTNode(CommandNodeType, result)
```

```python
def function_call_reco(self):
    if self.tokenType == WordTokType:
        term = ASTNode(TermNodeType, self.token)
        self.tokenType, self.token, self.lineNo = self.tokens.next()
        if self.tokenType == LParTokType:
            self.tokenType, self.token, self.lineNo = self.tokens.next()
            result = self.function_call_list_reco()
            if result:
                if self.tokenType == RParTokType:
                    self.tokenType, self.token, self.lineNo = \
                        self.tokens.next()
                    return ASTNode(FunctionCallNodeType, term, result)
                else:
                    raise ParseError(self.lineNo, 'missing right paren')
            else:
                raise ParseError(self.lineNo, 'bad function call list')
        else:
            raise ParseError(self.lineNo, ' misplaced left paren')
```

```python
        else:
            return none
    def function_call_list_reco(self):
        terms = []
        while 1:
            result = self.function_call_reco()
            if not result:
                break
            terms.append(result)
            if self.tokenType != CommaTokType:
                break
            self.tokenType, self.token, self.lineNo =
self.tokens.next()
        return ASTNode(FuncCallListNodeType, terms)
#
# The Parse error exception class.
#
class ParseError(Exception):
    def __init__ (self, lineNo, msg):
        RuntimeError.__init__(self, msg)
        self.lineNo = lineNo
        self.msg = msg
    def getLineNo(self):
```

```
        return self.lineNo
    def getMsg(self):
        return self.msg
def is word(token):
    for letter in token:
        if letter not in string.ascii_letters:
            return None
    return 1
#
# Generate the tokens.
# Usage:
#   gen = genTokens(infile)
#   tokType, tok, lineNo = gen.next()
#   ...
def genTokens(infile):
    lineNo = 0
    while 1:
        lineNo += 1
        try:
            line = infile.next()
        except:
            yield (EOFTokType, None, lineNo)
        toks = line.split()
```

```
    for tok in toks:
        if is_word(tok):
            tokType = WordTokType
        elif tok == '(':
            tokType = LParTokType
        elif tok == ')':
            tokType = RParTokType
        elif tok == ',':
            tokType = CommaTokType
        yield (tokType, tok, lineNo)
def test(infileName):
    parser = ProgParser()
    #ipshell('(test) #1\nCtrl-D to exit')
    result = None
    try:
        result = parser.parseFile(infileName)
    except ParseError, exp:
        sys.stderr.write('ParseError: (%d) %s\n' % \
            (exp.getLineNo(), exp.getMsg()))
    if result:
        result.show(0)
def usage():
    print __doc__
```

```python
    sys.exit(1)
def main():
  args = sys.argv[1:]
  try:
    opts, args = getopt.getopt(args, 'h', ['help'])
  except:
    usage()
  relink = 1
  for opt, val in opts:
    if opt in ('-h', '--help'):
      usage()
  if len(args) != 1:
    usage()
  inputfile = args[0]
  test(inputfile)
if __name__ == '__main__':
  #import pdb; pdb.set_trace()
  main()
```

Explanation:

The tokenizer Python generator sends back a generator that can provide the tokType, tok, and lineNo tuples. Our tokenizer is a simple-minded one; we separated every token using whitespace.

The parser class (ProgParser) have the recognizer

function that executes production rules. All these functions identify a syntactic construct that a rule describes. Our example stated that these functions contain names ending with "_reco".

We could have executed our recognizers as global functions, rather than methods in a class. Therefore, utilizing a class provides a place to "hang" the variables required across methods and saves us the time of having to use ("evil") global variables.

A recognizer function signifies terminals (syntactic syntax on the right of the grammar rule that has no grammar rule) by (1) examine the token type and value, (2) and calling the function to obtain the succeeding token (it consumed a token).

A recognizer function examines and operates on a non-terminal (syntactic syntax on the right that contains a grammar rule) by calling the recognizer

The functions of executing a non-terminal

If a recognizer function gets a syntax error, it outputs the class exception ParserError.

Remember our recursive descent parser example builds an AST (abstract syntax tree) when a recognizer function identifies a syntactic construct, it produces an instance of ASTNode class to stand for it and send back the same example to its caller. The ASTNode class contain a node type and has child nodes that are built by recognizer functions called by this one (i.e., that stand for nonterminal on the right of a grammar rule).

Every time a recognizer function "occupies a token," it calls tokenizer to obtain the succeeding token.

The tokenizer sends back a token type as well as the value of the token. Also, it sends back a line number for error details.

Build the syntax tree from instances of ASTNode class

The ASTNode class contain a show function, that accompanies the AST and provides output. The below code is a data sample we can use with this parser:

aaa ( )

bbb (ccc ( ))

ddd (eee ( ) , fff (ggg ( ) , hhh ( ) , iii ( )))

And, when we launch the parser on this input data, it outputs:

$ Python workbook045.py workbook045.data

Node -- Type ProgNodeType

  Node -- Type CommandNodeType

    Node -- Type FuncCallNodeType

      Node -- Type TermNodeType

        Child: aaa

      Node -- Type FuncCallListNodeType

  Node -- Type CommandNodeType

    Node -- Type FuncCallNodeType

      Node -- Type TermNodeType

Child: bbb

Node -- Type FuncCallListNodeType

Node -- Type FuncCallNodeType

Node -- Type TermNodeType

Child: ccc

Node -- Type FuncCallListNodeType

Node -- Type CommandNodeType

Node -- Type FuncCallNodeType

Node -- Type TermNodeType

Child: ddd

Node -- Type FuncCallListNodeType

Node -- Type FuncCallNodeType

Node -- Type TermNodeType

Child: eee

Node -- Type FuncCallListNodeType

Node -- Type FuncCallNodeType

Node -- Type TermNodeType

Child: fff

Node -- Type FuncCallListNodeType

Node -- Type FuncCallNodeType

Node -- Type TermNodeType

Child: ggg

Node -- Type FuncCallListNodeType

Node -- Type FuncCallNodeType

Node -- Type TermNodeType

Child: hhh

Node -- Type FuncCallListNodeType

Node -- Type FuncCallNodeType

Node -- Type TermNodeType

Child: iii

Node -- Type FuncCallListNodeType

Creating a parser with Pyparsing

Pyparsing is a brand-new package for Python, enforced by Paul McGuire. It is easy to utilize and functions perfectly for quick parsing tasks. It also contains attributes that make a few complex parsing operations very much easy. It uses the original Python style to build parsers.

Parsing comma delimited lines

This is a straightforward grammar for lines with fields differentiated by commas:

```
import sys

from pyparsing import alphanums, ZeroOrMore, Word

fieldDef = Word(alphanums)

lineDef = fieldDef + ZeroOrMore("," + fieldDef)

def test():

    args = sys.argv[1:]
```

```
    if len(args) != 1:

        print 'usage: Python pyparsing_test1.py
<datafile.txt>'

        sys.exit(-1)

    infilename = sys.argv[1]

    infile = file(infilename, 'r')

    for line in infile:

        fields = lineDef.parseString(line)

        print fields

test()
```

Here is some sample data:

abcd,defg

11111,22222,33333

Launching the parser on this data, it displays the following:

$ Python comma_parser.py sample1.data

['abcd', ',', 'defg']

['11111', ',', '22222', ',', '33333']

Explanation:

The grammar is built from primary Python calls to function and class/object constructors. I built the parser in-line because it is a straightforward example, but building the parser in a function, a module would work better for complex grammar. Pyparsing is easy to use in different styles.

Utilize "+" to indicate a succession.

Utilize ZeroOrMore to show iteration. In the sample, a lineDef is a fieldDef accompanied by zero or few fieldDef and commas. Utilize OneOrMore to demand one occurrence at least.

Parsing comma delimited text happens regularly; therefore, pyparsing offers a shortcut.

Replace:

lineDef = fieldDef + ZeroOrMore("," + fieldDef)

with:

lineDef = delimitedList(fieldDef)

DelimitedList takes an alternative argument of delim which is utilized to indicate the delimiter. A comma is the default.

Parsing functions

Our sample parses the form func(arg1, arg2, arg3) expressions:

Pyparsing inserts ZeroOrMore, Literal, alphas, Word, nums, alphanums.

lparen = Literal("(")

rparen = Literal(")")

identifier = Word(alphas, alphanums + "_")

integer = Word(nums)

functor = identifier

arg = identifier | integer

```
args = arg + ZeroOrMore("," + arg)
expression = functor + lparen + args + rparen
def test():
    content = raw input("Enter an expression: ")
    parsedContent = expression.parseString(content)
    print parsedContent
test()
```

Explanation:

- Utilize Literal to indicate an equally matched fixed string.
- Word would take an alternative second argument. With one string argument, it equals connecting words consisting of characters within the string. With double string arguments, it equals a word that its initial value is inside the first string, and the rest of its values are within the second string. So, the description of identifier equals a word that its initial value is an alpha and the rest of its values are alpha-numerics/underscores.
- Utilize a vertical bar for alternation. Our example illustrates that an arg can be an identifier or an integer.

We are parsing phone digits, names, etc.

To make an example of it, we will parse expressions with the below form:

Enter the below set-up:

[ID] [phone] [city, state, zip]

Last, first   000-222-3333 city, ca 444

Check the parser below:

```python
import sys

from pyparsing import alphas, Combine, Suppress,
Word, nums, Group, ZeroOrMore,

lastname = Word(alphas)

firstname = Word(alphas)

city         =          Group(Word(alphas)          +
ZeroOrMore(Word(alphas)))

state = Word(alphas, exact=2)

zip = Word(nums, exact=5)

name = Group(lastname + Suppress(",") + firstname)

phone = Combine(Word(nums, exact=3) + "-" +
Word(nums, exact=3) + "-"

+ Word(nums, exact=4))

location = Group(city + Suppress(",") + state + zip)

record = name + phone + location

def test():

  args = sys.argv[1:]

  if len(args) != 1:

    print  'usage:   Python   pyparsing_test3.py
<datafile.txt>'

    sys.exit(-1)

  infilename = sys.argv[1]
```

```
infile = file(infilename, 'r')
for line in infile:
    line = line.strip()
    if line and line[0] != "#":
        fields = record.parseString(line)
        print fields
test()
```

And, here is some sample input:

Louderdal, Jerry   111-222-3333   Bakersfield, CA
95111

Kacker, Katy   111-222-3334   Fresno, CA 95112

Kerry, Larrymoore   111-222-5135   Los Angeles, CA
94001

The above parsing input will output the following:

[['Jabberer', 'Jerry'], '111-222-3333', [['Bakersfield'],
'CA',

'95111']]

[['Kacker', 'Kerry'], '111-222-3334', [['Fresno'], 'CA',
'45312']]

[['Louderdal', 'Larrymoore'], '111-222-3335', [['Los',
'Angeles'], 'CA',

'64401']]

Comments:

We utilized the len=n argument to the Word
constructor to stop the parser to receiving a particular

47

number of characters, for instance within the zip code and phone digits. Word allows min=n" and ``max=n to stop the word length in a range.

We utilized Group to group parsed results to sub-lists, for instance, in the city and name description. The group allows you to arrange parse results to straightforward parse trees.

We utilized Combine to connect parsed results to one string. For instance, the phone number requires dashes and still link the results back to one string.

We utilized Suppress to detach unwanted sub-elements from the parsed results. For instance, a comma is unwanted between first and last names.

Functions and Debugging

The def statement describes functions and methods. The def statement is offering a function or method, and the statement attaches it to a variable within the contemporary name-space.

Recommendations: (1) Utilize Python code checker, for instance, pylint or flake8; (2) Conduct a thorough test and utilize the Python framework. Pythonic wisdom: If you fail to test it, it becomes broken.

Returning values

Utilize the statement to send back values from a function.

The return statement holds values differentiated by commas. Utilizing commas will send back one tuple.

None is its default value.

To send back various values, utilize a list or tuple. Remember that unpacking (assignment) is used to apprehend several values. Sending back various items differentiated by commas is equal to sending back a tuple. Example:

```
In [8]: def test(x, y):
   ...:     return x * 3, y * 4
   ...:
In [9]: a, b = test(3, 4)
In [10]: print a
9
In [11]: print b
16
In [53]: def t(max=5):
   ....:     for val in range(max):
   ....:         print val
   ....:
   ....:
In [54]: t(3)
0
1
2
In [55]: t()
0
```

1

2

3

4

Setting a parameter, a default value enables the parameter become optional.

Note: When a function contains a parameter that has a default value, and every typical argument should move the parameters containing default values. More completely, set parameters from left to right in this order:

1. Normal arguments.
2. Arguments are containing default values.
3. The argument list (*args).
4. Keyword arguments (**kwargs).

List parameters -- *args. It's a tuple.

Keyword parameters -- **kwargs. It's a dictionary.

Arguments

When you call a function, values could go to the function that possesses positional or keyword arguments.

Place positional arguments ahead of the keyword arguments (to the left of).

Transferring lists to a function as several arguments. This syntax some_func(*aList) lets Python unfold arguments. Example:

```
def fn1(*args, **kwargs):
```

fn2(*args, **kwargs)

Local variables

Create local variables - A bind operation develops a local variable. Samples are (1) function parameters; (2) the import statement; etc. The opposite of accessing a variable.

The Global Statement

Within a function, utilize global while setting the global variable's value. Example:

def fn():

    global   Some_global_variable, Another_global_variable

    Some_global_variable = 'hello'

More things about functions

Functions are high class. You can save functions within a structure, give them a function, and send them back from a function.

- Function calls hold keyword arguments. For instance:
  - \>>> test(size=25)

- Functions formal parameters can contain default values. For instance:
  - \>>> def test(size=0):

- Don't utilize mutable objects to become default values.

- You can apprehend the rest of the arguments with **kwargs and *args. For instance:

In [13]: def test(size, *args, **kwargs):

print size

print args

print kwargs

In [14]: test(40, 'xx', 'cc', otherparam='ppy')

40

('xx', 'cc')

{'otherparam': 'ppy'}

- You should utilize normal arguments ahead of default arguments that come before keyword arguments.
- A function without a value sends back None.
- To determine a global variable value, proclaim that variable with the global statement.

Assignment within a method or function develops a local variable.

Cite variables, evaluate local variables if the variable has been developed, to assess a global variable. To attach values to global variables, proclaim variables as global from the start of the method and function.

If within a method or function, you cite and proclaim a variable, you should either:

1. Proclaim the variable first.
2. Proclaim variable as global.

The global statement Proclaims variables (one or more), differentiated by commas, to become global.

Some examples:

```
In [1]:
In [1]: X = 3
In [2]: def t():
   ...:     print X
   ...:
In [3]:
In [3]: t()
3
In [4]: def s():
   ...:     X = 4
   ...:
In [5]:
In [5]:
In [5]: s()
In [6]: t()
3
In [7]: X = -1
In [8]: def u():
   ...:     global X
   ...:     X = 5
   ...:
In [9]:
```

In [9]: u()

In [10]: t()

5

In [16]: def v():

....:   x = X

....:   X = 6

....:   return x

....:

In [17]:

In [17]: v()

Traceback (most recent call last):

  File "<ipython console>", line 1, in <module>

  File "<ipython console>", line 2, in v

UnboundLocalError: local variable 'X' cited ahead of the assignment

In [18]: def w():

....:   global X

....:   x = X

....:   X = 7

....:   return x

....:

In [19]:

In [19]: w()

Out[19]: 5

In [20]: X

Out[20]: 7

Doc strings for functions

Attach doc strings to be a triple-quoted string starting with the opening line of a method and function.

Decorators for functions

A decorator conducts modification on a function. Decorators samples, which are in-built functions, are as follows: @classmethod, @staticmethod, and @property.

A decorator is used through the "@" character on a line before the function header definition. Examples:

```
class SomeClass(object):
    @classmethod
    def HelloClass(cls, arg):
        pass
    ## HelloClass = classmethod(HelloClass)
    @staticmethod
    def HelloStatic(arg):
        pass
    ## HelloStatic = staticmethod(HelloStatic)
#
```

```
# Define/implement a decorator.
def wrapper(fn):
    def inner_fn(*args, **kwargs):
        print '>>'
        result = fn(*args, **kwargs)
        print '<<'
        return result
    return inner_fn
#
# Apply a decorator.
@wrapper
def fn1(msg):
    pass
## fn1 = wrapper(fn1)
```

Notes:

- The decorator form containing the "@" character is equal to forms that call decorator function directly.
- Execute a decorator as a function. So, to understand some particular decorator, find the attestation or the execution of that function. To utilize a function, define it in the existing module.
- The form that calls the decorator function calls directly is equal to the form utilizing the "@" character.

Lambda

Utilize Lambda as comfort when the function needed is both:

- Anonymous (do not require a name), AND
- Lambda has expression without a statement.

Sample:

In [1]: fn = lambda a, y, z: (x ** 2) + (y * 2) + z

In [2]: fn(4, 5, 6)

Out[2]: 32

In [3]: format = lambda obj, group: 'Our "%s" looks like "%s".' % (obj, group)

In [4]: format('pine houses', 'conifer')

Out[4]: 'The "pine houses" is a "conifer".'

A lambda can hold several arguments and can send several values like a function.

Example:

In [79]: a = lambda x, y: (a * 3, y * 4, (x, y))

In [80]:

In [81]: a(3, 4)

Out[81]: (9, 16, (3, 4))

Suggestion: In few instances, you can utilize a lambda as an event handler.

Sample:

class Test:

```python
def __init__ (self, first='', last=''):
    self.first = first
    self.last = last
def test(self, formatter):
    """
```

Test for lambdas

Formatter is a function that takes two arguments, first and last names, and should return the formatted name.

```python
    """
    msg = 'My nick is %s' % (formatter(self.begin, self.last),)
    print message
def test():
    t = Test('Dave', 'katy')
t.test(lambda begin, last: '%s %s' % (begin, end ))
    t.test(lambda begin, last: '%s, %s' % (last, begin, ))
test()
```

Lambda let you describe functions where names are not required for functions. Sample:

```python
In [45]: a = [
    ....: lambda x: x,
    ....: lambda x: x * 2,
    ....: ]
```

In [46]:

In [46]: a

Out[46]: [<function __main__.<lambda>>, <function __main__.<lambda>>]

In [47]: a[0](3)

Out[47]: 3

In [48]: a[1](3)

Out[48]: 6

Iterators and generators iterator

The iterator pleases iterator protocols. You can utilize the iterator in a For statement.

Generator

A generator is a function or class that executes an iterator protocol.

The iterator protocols

An object pleases the iterator protocol when it performs the following:

Executes an __iter__ method, that sends back an iterator object.

Executes the next function, that sends back the succeeding item from the group, secession, stream, and so on to get iterated over.

It lifts the StopIteration exception by the time the items drains and then calls the next() method.

Yield

It is the yield statement that lets us write functions that are generators. These types of functions are likened to co-routines because they could "yield" several times. Yield is an expression. A method or function that has a yield statement executes a generator. Attaching yield statements to methods or function transforms that method or function into one that when you call it, it sends back a generator, i.e., Objects that execute the iterator protocol. A generator offers a comforting way to execute a filter. Consider:

- The filter() in-built function.
- List comprehensions using the If clause.

Below are a few samples:

```
def simplegenerator():
    yield 'aaa'              # Note 1
    yield 'bbb.'
    yield 'ccc.'
def list_tripler(somelist):
    for the item in somelist:
        item *= 3
        yield item
def limit_iterator(somelist, max):
    for the item in somelist:
        if item > max:
            return          # Note 2
```

```python
        yield item
def test():
    print '1.', '-' * 30
    it = simplegenerator()
    for the item in it:
        print item
    print '2.', '-' * 30
    alist = range(5)
    it = list_tripler(alist)
    for the item in it:
        print item
    print '3.', '-' * 30
    alist = range(8)
  it = limit_iterator(alist, 4)
    for item in it:
        print item
    print '4.', '-' * 30
    it = simplegenerator()
    try:
        print it.next()          # Note 3
        print it.next()
        print it.next()
        print it.next()
```

61

```
    except StopIteration, exp:        # Note 4
        print 'reached the end of sequence'
if __name__ == '__main__':
    test()
```
Notes:

1. Yield statements send back a value. When you request the following item and resume implementation does not stop after the yield statement.
2. We can discontinue the successions initiated by an iterator through a return statement containing no value.
3. To continue a generator, utilize its send() or next() methods. Send () works like next(), but offer values to the yield expression.
4. We can also acquire the items within a succession by calling iterator's next() method. Because iterators are high-class objects, you can store it inside a data structure and can send around for utilization at various times and locations within our program.
5. When an iterator drains, it outputs the StopIteration exception.

Below is the output from launching the sample above:

$ Python test_iterator.py

1. -----------------------------

aaa

bbb

ccc

2. -----------------------------

0

3

6

9

12

3. -----------------------------

0

1

2

3

4

4. -----------------------------

aaa

bbb

ccc

reached end of the sequence

An instance of a class that executes the __iter__ method, sending back an iterator, is iterable (e.g., utilize it in a for statement or within a comprehension list, or inside the generator expression, or to be an argument to iter() in-built method). But, the class will execute a generator method that you can call directly.

Examples

The below code executes an iterator that provides every object within a chain of objects:

```
class Node:
    def __init__ (me, data, pupils=None):
        me.initlevel = 0
        me.data = data
        if pupils are None:
            me. pupils = []
        else:
            me. pupils = pupils
    def set_initlevel(self, initlevel): me.initlevel = initlevel
    def get_initlevel(self): return self.initlevel
    def addchild(self, child):
        me.pupils.append(child)
    def get data(me):
        return me.data
    def get pupils(me):
        return me.pupils
    def show chain(me, level):
        me.show_level(level)
        print 'data: %s' % (me.data)
        for child in me.pupils:
```

```
        child.show_chain(level + 1)
    def show level(me, level):
        print ' ' * level,
    #
    # The generator method #1
    # The generator transforms this class examples to
iterable objects.
    #
    def walk chain(self, level):
        yield (class, self,)
        for child in self.get_children():
            for class1, chain1 in child.walk_chain(class+1):
                yield class1, chain1
    def __iter__(self):
        return self.walk_chain(self.initlevel)
#
# The generator method #2
# The generator utilizes the support function
(walk_list).
#
def walk_chain(chain, class):
    yield (class, chain)
    for child in walk_list(chain.get_children(),
    class+1):
```

```
      yield child
def walk_list(chain, class):
   for tree in chain:
      for tree in walk_chain(chain, class):
         yield chain
#
# The generator method #3
# This generator is similar to method #2, but called as
an (iterator), instead of calling support functions.
#
def walk_chain_recur(tree, level):
   yield (level, chain,)
   for child in chain.get_children():
      for class1, tree1 in walk_chain_recur(child,
class+1):
         yield (class1, chain1)
def show_class(class):
   print ' ' * class,
def test():
   a7 = Node('777')
   a6 = Node('666')
   a5 = Node('555')
   a4 = Node('444')
```

```
a3 = Node('333', [a4, a5])
a2 = Node('222', [a6, a7])
a1 = Node('111', [a2, a3])
initLevel = 2
a1.show_chain(initClass)
print '=' * 40
for level, item in walk_chain(a1, initClass):
    show_level(class)
    print 'item:', item.get_data()
print '=' * 40
for class, item in walk_chain_recur(a1, initClass):
    show_class(class)
    print 'item:', item.get_data()
print '=' * 40
a1.set_initclass(initClass)
for class, item in a1:
    show_level(class)
    print 'item:', item.get_data()
iter1 = iter(a1)
print iter1
print iter1.next()
print iter1.next()
print iter1.next()
```

```
    print iter1.next()

    print iter1.next()

    print iter1.next()

    print iter1.next()

##   print iter1.next()

    return a1

if __name__ == '__main__':

    test()
```

Notes:

- A class Node instance is "iterable." Utilize it in a For statement, list comprehensions, and so on. Therefore, for instance, when you use a node instance within the for statement, it outputs an iterator.
- You can as well call the Node.walk_method in a direct to acquire an iterator.
- Method Node.walk_tree, walk_tree_recur, and functions walk tree are generators. When you call any of them, it sends back an iterator because each has a yield statement.
- These functions or methods are recursive. Each one can call itself.

Debugging tools pdb --

This is the debugger for Python:

- Launch the debugger by creating an expression:

pdb.run('expression')

Example:

```
if __name__ == '__main__':
    import pdb
    pdb.run('main()')
```

- Launch the debugger at a particular position using the below code:

```
import pdb; pdb.set_trace()
```

Example:

```
if __name__ == '__main__':
    import pdb
    pdb.set_trace()
    main()
```

- Obtain assistance from inside the debugger. For instance:

```
(Pdb) help
```

```
(Pdb) help next
```

IPython can also be embedded into your code.

ipdb - Ipdb debugger interactive prompt contains few additional characteristics, for instance, its complete tab names.

Inspecting:

- import inspect
- Also try dir(obj) and type(obj) and help(obj), first.

Miscellaneous tools:

- id(obj)
- globals() and locals().
- dir(obj) -- Sends back wonderful names, but the list may not be complete.
- obj.__class__
- cls.__bases__
- obj.__class__.__bases__
- obj.__doc__. But often, help(obj) performs better. It outputs the doc string.

Customize your class representation. Describe these methods inside your class:

- __repr__() -- Called by (1) repr(), (2) interactive interpreter when it needs representation.
- __str__() -- Called by (1) str(), (2) string formatting.

You can execute **PDB** through cmd module within Python standard library, and cmd can also implement comparable command-line interfaces.

Chapter 3:
GUI Applications

Your GUI needs can be a minimalist (one or two pop-up dialogs), and if your application is compulsory instead of being for events, you may have to contemplate the EasyGUI option. Just as its name sounds, it is easy to use.

EasyGUI applications

You would know that you can utilize EasyGUI when:

- You do not need windows that have menus and menu bar to run your application.
- Your GUI requires a bit more than showing a dialog every time to receive answers from the user.
- You want to write a non-event driven app, an app that your code rests and awaits the user to begin operation.

EasyGUI offers functions for several frequently required dialog boxes like:

- Enter enables the entrance of a line of text.
- An integer box allows entry of an integer.

A simple EasyGUI sample

This sample induces the user for entry, and displays the reply within the message box:

import easygui

```
def testeasygui():

    response      =      easygui.enterbox(msg='input
name:'title='Name Entry')

    easygui.msgbox(msg=response,           title='Your
Response')

testeasygui()
```

An EasyGUI file sample to open dialog

This example introduces a dialog permitting the user to choose a file:

```
import easygui

def test():

    response = easygui.fileopenbox(msg='Select a file')

    print 'filename: %s' % response

test()
```

Guidance on Packages and Modules

The Python programming language has an excellent range of execution operation structures. They span from the statements structure to control structures utilizing functions, classes, methods, packages, and modules at a higher level.

Python package is a group of Python modules within a disk index. It can bring in single modules from the index, and the index should have a file named __init__.py. (this does not apply to indexes in PYTHONPATH.) The __init__.py serves a few purposes:

- The file __init__.py presence in an index signifies the index as a Python package, which allows modules importation from the index.
- The first time an application import module from the directory, evaluate the code in the module __init__.

Utilizing Packages

One way to allow users to bring in and use a package is to command the act of importing individual modules from the package.

The second is an improved way to allow users to bring in the package is to uncover those package attributes in the __init__ module. If module mod2 has functions fun2a and fun3b and if module mod3 has functions fun2a and fun3b, then file __init__.py might contain the following:

from mod2 import fun2a, fun3b

from mod3 import fun2a, fun3b

Then, if you access the following in the user's code:

    import testpackages

The testpackages will accommodate fun2a, fun3b, fun2a, and fun3b.

For instance, below is an illustration that display importing the package:

>>> import testpackages

>>> print dir(testpackages)

[`__builtins__', `__doc__', `__files__',

`__names__',

`__path__',

`fun2a', `fun3b', `fun2a', `fun3b', `mod2', `mod3']

Sharing and Installing Packages

Python Distribution Utilities (Distutils) provides outstanding support for sharing and installing packages.

Here is an example, think of having an index with the following:

Testpackages

Testpackages/README

Testpackages/MANIFEST.in

Testpackages/setup.py

Testpackages/testpackages/__init__.py

Testpackages/testpackages/mod1.py

Testpackages/testpackages/mod2.py

The sub-directory Testpackages/testpackages has the file __init__.py. This Python package is the one to install.

We'll explain the configuration of the files above so that you can package them as one distribution file and obtain the package in them as a package by Distutils.

MANIFEST.in file lists files that we will incorporate in our distribution. The contents of MANIFEST.in file is:

include README MANIFEST MANIFEST.in

include setup.py

include testpackages/*.py

The setup.py file narrates to Distutils how to package and installation distribution files. The contents of setup.py are:

```
#!/usr/bin/env Python

from distutils.core import setup          # [1]

long_description = 'Tests for installing and sharing
Python packages'

setup(name = 'testpackages',              # [2]

    version = '1.0a',

    description = 'Tests for Python packages',

    maintainer = 'Dave katy',

    maintainer_email = 'dkaty@rexx.com',

    URL = 'http://www.rexx.com/~dkaty',

    long_description = long_description,

    packages = ['testpackages']           # [3]

    )
```

Explanation:

1. First, we import important elements from Distutils.

2. We narrate the package and its maintainer.

3. We indicate the index that will install as a package.

When the distribution is installed by the user, the index and every module it contains will install as a package.

To build a distribution file, run the below code:

Python setup.py sdist --formats=gztar

It creates a file testpackages-1.0a.tar.gz under the index dist.

Then, install this distribution file by performing the following:

$ tar xvzf testpackages-1.0a.tar.gz

$ cd testpackages-1.0a

$ Python setup.py build

$ Python setup.py install   # as root

Chapter 4:
Introduction to C, C++, C#

C is a programming language developed at AT&T's Bell Laboratories of the United States of America in 1972. Dennis Ritchie wrote the language. C came into existence for a particular reason, which was to design the UNIX operating system. A lot of computers utilize this system. C++ is a language developed by Bjarne Stroustrup to become a C programming language extension. The language has grown severely with time, and now contains generic, object-oriented, and functional attributes as well as provisions for low-level memory control. It executes as a compiled language, and a lot of vendors offer C++ compilers, together with the Free Software Foundation, Microsoft, etc. C++ is also very useful in software substructure applications as well as desktop applications, servers, etc. The initial developers of C# programming languages are Eric Gunnerson, Peter Golde, Peter Sollichy, Anders Hejlsberg, and Scott Wiltamuth. The architect of the C# language is Anders Hejlsberg, a lead developer at Microsoft in 2000. C# came into existence as an object-oriented programming language.

Data Types and Sizes

Regular data types in programming languages are called primitive types such as integers, characters, floating-point numbers, and so on. In C, C++, and C#. you should declare every variable before you use them, generally at the start of the function before statement execution.

C

C programming consists of four necessary date types.

- int ---- "an integer, generally displays the sizes of the integer on the host machine."
- float --- "single-precision floating-point."
- double --- "double-precision floating-point."
- char --- "a single byte, can hold a single character in the local character set."

C programming consists of five types of Specifiers. They are:

long

long long

short

unsigned

signed

You cannot abbreviate or utilize the C language reserved keywords. The C language reserved keywords are: auto, else, long, switch, break, enum, register, typedef, case, extern, return, union, char, float, short, unsigned, const, for, signed, void, continue, goto, sizeof, volatile, default, if, static, while, do, int, struct, _Packed, double.

In C, all data types, like an integer, character, or floating-point number, contain a series of related values. Determine the value by the storage size assigned to store a specific data type within the computer memory. Storage sizes depend on your type of device. This attribute is termed "machine-dependent." For instance, an integer can occupy 32 bits on your device, or you could save it in 64 bits on another device.

C++

The C++ basic data types are identical to C. C++ also has one more type called Boolean. A Boolean can contain any of the true or false values. Express logical operations result with the use of Boolean.

C and C++ together contain 32 keywords. They are auto, else, long, switch, break, enum, register, typedef, case, extern, return, union, char, float, short, unsigned, const, for, signed, void, continue, goto, sizeof, volatile, default, if, static, while, do, int, struct, and double.

C++ does not use the keyword _Packed anymore.

C++ utilizes 30 keywords that C does not.

New keywords in C++:

Asm, dynamic cast, namespace, reinterpret_cast, bool, explicit, new, static_cast, catch, false, operator, template, class, friend, private, this, const_cast, inline, public, throw, delete, mutable, protected, true, try, typeid, typename, using, virtual, wchar_t.

C#

The C# Boolean type has a slight difference with C++. In C#, assign only two values to the Boolean type, which is true or false. While in C++, you can also assign 0 as the value to the Boolean type, which means false, and the rest means true.

Another difference between C# and C++ is integral Types. In C and C++, there is only one type for the integral type. While in C#, an integral is a group of types like the char type, it is signed or unsigned.

C# contains much more keywords than C and C++. It includes a total of 87 reserved words. All the keywords in C# are:

Abstract, as, base, bool, break by 2, byte, case, catch, char, checked, class, const, continue, decimal, default, delegate, do, double, descending 2, explicit, event, extern, else, enum, false, finally, fixed, float, for, foreach, from 2, goto, group 2, if implicit, in, int, interface, internal, into 2, is, lock, long, new, null, namespace, object, operator, out, override, orderby 2, params, private, protected, public, read-only, ref, return, switch, struct, sbyte, sealed, short, sizeof, stackalloc, static, string, select 2, this, throw, true, try, typeof, uint, ulong, unchecked, unsafe, ushort, using, var 2, virtual, volatile, void, while, where 2, yield 1.

String type

The c programming language has no string type. Therefore, the char type of array replaces it. C++

programming language contains strings of two types, C-style and C++-style strings. A C-style string includes an array of characters stopped by the null character '\0', and its properties are above a regular array of characters. It also consists of a collection of functions to handle strings. A 'class' data type, that is how to define C++ style string. The C++ style string objects are examples of the C++ 'string' class. There is a collection of C++ string functions too.

Structure

There are two differences in the structure of C and C++ language.

1. C Structure consists of data items only, and C++ structure can include functions and data.
2. Utilizing the 'struct' keyword in the C language is required to build a variable. While in C++, you need the structure name only to locate a variable.

There is a significant difference in the structures of C++ and C#. In C++, a struct is similar to a class, only if the default access and inheritance are public instead of being private. While in C#, structs are different right from classes. C# Structs are developed to summarize insubstantial objects. Structs are value types. Therefore, they pass by value. Structs have restrictions which cannot attach to classes. For instance, they cannot be obtained from or contain base class except System.ValueType which it got from Object. Structs also do not proclaim a parameterless constructor, but they are appropriate for utilizing a class containing a little sample and are very productive, more than classes, which makes them very good for insubstantial objects development.

Inherence

Inherence means developing a new class obtained from the running class. The derived class gets every method and variables from the base class. Predominant properties and methods can enlarge the operations of a base class. C programming language does not recognize inheritance as the language is not object-oriented. C# or Java do not allow several inheritances, which means one class can inherit only one class. C++ aids various classes of inheritance. In C++, classes and structs are very similar. Structs in C# do not aid inheritance and don't assist direct default constructors while C++ structs aid various inheritances.

Array

Every subarray with several dimensional arrays should consist of similar dimensions in C and C++. In C#, arrays don't need to be equal as building jagged arrays as a single-dimensional array of arrays. The array contents are arrays that could accommodate examples of references or type to the rest of the arrays. Jagged and multidimensional arrays are quite different in C#. Multidimensional arrays in C and C++ are similar, which adjoins block with members of the same type.

Reference and Value Types

The basic types of primitive data types like short, byte, long, int, double, float, char, Boolean. Reference types are creatable classes and arrays like Scanner, String, Die, Random, String[], int[], etc. Value and reference types are quite different in C#. Primitive and reference types are the same with Simple types like long, int, double, etc. While the value type in C# are structs.

Pointer

A variable that has another variable address is a pointer. In C and C++, you can use it as Strings, arrays, codable function parameters. While in C# pointer can be proclaimed to accommodate array and value types memory address.

Partial classes

C# permit class definition to be divided over various source files though the partial classes attribute. Mark every part with the partial keyword. C and C++ do not possess this function. In C++, utilize inheritance to attain the same goal.

Chapter 5:
What Is HTML?

Hypertext Markup Language (HTML) is the universal language for a one or several page project or documents developed to appear on a browser. Other languages support the HTML language such as JavaScript and Cascading Style Sheets (CSS). The browsers obtain HTML documents through the local storage or web server and then turn the file or document to multimedia pages. The structure of a page is defined by HTML in an informative manner and attach indications for the file presentation. HTML contains several elements, which are the development blocks of the language pages. HTML permits the insertion of different objects like tables, images, videos, and so on. The language also consists of different structural text semantics like paragraphs, headings, links, list, etc. HTML files are text files. Therefore, you can utilize various programs to build them like Sublime Text, Notepad++, Aptana, etc.

Anatomy of an HTML tag

Every tag in HTML programming language contains an opening and closing tag, and few contents between the tags as well as other elective attributes. Tags behave in a container manner. They give hints about data between the opening tags and closing tags.

```
<tagname atr1="val1"
atr2="val2">contents</tagname>
```

```
<tagname atr1="val1" atr2="val2">
```

Attribute

Attributes produce more information about elements contents. They are regularly placed on an element opening tag and consists of two parts: a name then a value, differentiated with an equal sign.

Basic structure of HTML

```
<!DOCTYPE html>
```

```
<html lang="en">
```

```
<head>
```

```
<meta charset="utf-8" />
```

```
<title>Page Title</title>
```

```
</head>
```

```
<body>
```

```
</body>
```

```
</html>
```

Doctype and HTML tag

The doctype is not a tag in particular, but it should be at the beginning of all HTML page to instruct the browser on what HTML version you're using. The <!DOCTYPE> is not a case sensitive declaration. The language attribute is often attached to the opening HTML tag. The attribute is utilized to indicate an element or page language. This assists Google to interpret your page languages.

Code:

```
<!DOCTYPE html>
<html lang="en">
</html> Head
```

The head carries the "meta" data regarding the page, data the browser needs commences operation. This head carries data regarding the page and not the data displayed within the major section of the browser window. A <title> element is always within the <head> element.

Meta tag

The meta tag is utilized to produce a page's data, and the data may be a short page description, page author, page keywords, etc. There are lots of meta tags.

Code:

```
<meta charset="utf-8" />
```

The above meta is utilized to determine your web page character encoding. We have several types of character encoding, and Unicode character encoding is the general choice for character encoding. Unicode has characters for several languages and assists on a lot of operating systems. Unicode shows various languages inside a page.

Title tag

The <title> element content displays in the browser top, in the URL section of the page, or on that page tab.

Code:

<title>page Title</title>

Create an HTML file

1. Launch the text editor, proceed to file, and select new or tap CTRL + N.
2. Go to the Save As box on the pop up and insert your file name accompanied with the file extension .html.
3. If there is more than a single word, differentiate them with the hyphen "--," do not utilize space.

Adding text to your web page

Text is attached to a web page utilizing the following:

Paragraph

Utilize the <p> tag to develop a paragraph within HTML, to build a paragraph, place your contents within the paragraph tag, which are the opening and closing tag. The browser displays every paragraph on a new line, adding few spaces to it.

HTML

<body>

<p>

A paragraph contains a single or more sentences that create an individual unit of dialogue. The beginning of a paragraph is signified by a new line

</p>

<p>

Texts are easily understood when they are divided into bits of text. For instance, a book could contain several chapters. Chapters may contain subheadings where you can attach one or more paragraphs.

</p>

</body>

Headings

HTML programming language contains six "levels" of headings.

Utilize <h1> for main headings, utilize <h2> for subheadings and when there are additional sections within the subheadings, utilize the <h3> element, and so on. Web browsers show contents of headings in various sizes. The <h1> element contents are the biggest, and the smallest is the <h6> element. Sizes the headings are displayed by the browser can vary. Below is an example:

HTML

<body>

<h1> Main Heading</h1>

<h2> Level 2 Heading</h2>

<h3> Level 3 Heading</h3>

<h4> Level 4 Heading</h4>

<h5> Level 5 Heading</h5>

<h6> Level 5 Heading</h6>

</body>

HTML

<h1>Welcome to this outstanding website, how can we help you?</h1>

<h2>Define html</h2>

<p>

Lorem ad minim veniam, quis nostrud exercitation ipsum dolor sit amet, consectetur adipiscing elit, sed do eiusmod dolore eu fugiat nulla. Ut enimullamco commodo reprehenderit consequat. Duis aute irure dolor in in voluptate velit laboris nisi ut aliquip ex ea esse cillum tempor incididunt ut pariaturlabore et dolore magna aliqua. </p>

<h3>Different types of HTML tags</h3>

<p>

Lorem ad minim veniam, quis nostrud exercitation ipsum dolor sit amet, consectetur adipiscing elit, sed do eiusmod dolore eu fugiat nulla. Ut enimullamco commodo reprehenderit consequat. Duis aute irure dolor in in voluptate velit laboris nisi ut aliquip ex ea esse cillum tempor incididunt ut pariaturlabore et dolore magna aliqua</p>

<h2>Define CSS</h2>

<p>

Lorem ad minim veniam, quis nostrud exercitation ipsum dolor sit amet, consectetur adipiscing elit, sed do eiusmod dolore eu fugiat nulla. Ut enimullamco commodo reprehenderit consequat. Duis aute irure dolor in in voluptate velit laboris nisi ut aliquip ex ea esse cillum tempor incididunt ut pariaturlabore et dolore magna aliqua</p>

<h3>Determine CSS selectors</h3>

<p>

Lorem ad minim veniam, quis nostrud exercitation ipsum dolor sit amet, consectetur adipiscing elit, sed do eiusmod dolore eu fugiat nulla. Ut enimullamco commodo reprehenderit consequat. Duis aute irure dolor in in voluptate velit laboris nisi ut aliquip ex ea esse cillum tempor incididunt ut pariaturlabore et dolore magna aliqua</p>

White space

If there are a lot of spaces on the text editor the web browser handles it as one space. When it finds a line break, it handles it as one-line space. You can call this process white space collapsing.

HTML

<body>

<h1>White space</h1>

<h2>Without white space</h2>

<p>The browser ignores white like this</p>

<h2>With spaces</h2>

<p>The browser will display this   white space

</p>

<h2>Browser ignores line spaces</h2>

<p>The browser will disregard this line spaces '

</p>

</body>

Line Breaks

Utilize this tag <br> to build a line break while using HTML.

HTML

<body>

<p>The world
gets two thousand tons every day
 because of the space dust.

</p>

</body>

Horizontal Rule

Utilize the <h> to build a long horizontal line

HTML

<p>

Lorem ad minim veniam, quis nostrud exercitation ipsum dolor sit amet, consectetur adipiscing elit, sed do eiusmod dolore eu fugiat nulla. Ut enimullamco commodo reprehenderit consequat. Duis aute irure dolor in in voluptate velit laboris nisi ut aliquip ex ea esse cillum tempor incididunt ut pariaturlabore et dolore magna aliqua </p>

<p>

Lorem ad minim veniam, quis nostrud exercitation ipsum dolor sit amet, consectetur adipiscing elit, sed do eiusmod dolore eu fugiat nulla. Ut enimullamco commodo reprehenderit consequat. Duis aute irure dolor in in voluptate velit laboris nisi ut aliquip ex ea esse cillum tempor incididunt ut pariaturlabore et dolore magna aliqua</p>

<p>

Lorem ad minim veniam, quis nostrud exercitation ipsum dolor sit amet, consectetur adipiscing elit, sed do eiusmod dolore eu fugiat nulla. Ut enimullamco commodo reprehenderit consequat. Duis aute irure dolor in in voluptate velit laboris nisi ut aliquip ex ea esse cillum tempor incididunt ut pariaturlabore et dolore magna aliqua</p>

<hr>

<p>

Lorem ad minim veniam, quis nostrud exercitation ipsum dolor sit amet, consectetur adipiscing elit, sed do eiusmod dolore eu fugiat nulla. Ut enimullamco commodo reprehenderit consequat. Duis aute irure dolor in in voluptate velit laboris nisi ut aliquip ex ea esse cillum tempor incididunt ut pariaturlabore et dolore magna aliqua </p>

<p>

Lorem ad minim veniam, quis nostrud exercitation ipsum dolor sit amet, consectetur adipiscing elit, sed do eiusmod dolore eu fugiat nulla. Ut enimullamco commodo reprehenderit consequat. Duis aute irure dolor in in voluptate velit laboris nisi ut aliquip ex ea esse cillum tempor incididunt ut pariaturlabore et dolore magna aliqua</p>

<p>

Lorem ad minim veniam, quis nostrud exercitation ipsum dolor sit amet, consectetur adipiscing elit, sed do eiusmod dolore eu fugiat nulla. Ut enimullamco commodo reprehenderit consequat. Duis aute irure dolor in in voluptate velit laboris nisi ut aliquip ex ea esse cillum tempor incididunt ut pariaturlabore et dolore magna aliqua</p>

Strong tag

The <strong> element signifies content of solid significance. For instance, the content within this element could be used with strong emphasis. Browsers displays the texts of a <strong> element in bold format. This attribute primary use is to bolden texts.

HTML

<p>

<strong>Beware:</strong> Beware of women this area.

</p>

<p>

I'm thinking of heading to Germany <strong> but I cannot find my passport.

</strong>

</p>

Quotations

You can utilize these two elements for quotations marking: The <q> element and <blockquote>.

<blockquote>

The <blockquote> element is utilized for larger quotes which takes a whole paragraph. Browsers would align the <blockquote> element text. Do not utilize this element to align just contents instead utilize CSS.

HTML

<p>

Lorem ad minim veniam, quis nostrud exercitation Ipsum dolor sit amet, consectetur adipiscing elit, sed do eiusmod dolore eu fugiat nulla. Ut enimullamco commodo reprehenderit consequat. Duis aute irure dolor in voluptate velit laboris nisi ut aliquip ex ea esse cillum tempor incididunt ut pariaturlabore et dolore Magna aliqua</p>

<blockquote cite="http:/www.google.com/ ">

<p>

Lorem ad minim veniam, quis nostrud exercitation Ipsum dolor sit amet, consectetur adipiscing elit, sed do eiusmod dolore eu fugiat nulla. Ut enimullamco commodo reprehenderit consequat. Duis aute irure dolor in voluptate velit laboris nisi ut aliquip ex ea esse cillum tempor incididunt ut pariaturlabore et dolore Magna aliqua</p>

</blockquote>

```
<p>
```

Lorem ad minim veniam, quis nostrud exercitation Ipsum dolor sit amet, consectetur adipiscing elit, sed do eiusmod dolore eu fugiat nulla. Ut enimullamco commodo reprehenderit consequat. Duis aute irure dolor in voluptate velit laboris nisi ut aliquip ex ea esse cillum tempor incididunt ut pariaturlabore et dolore Magna aliqua.

```
</p>
```

```
<q>
```

Utilize the <q> element for smaller quotes that are inside a paragraph. Browsers should place quotes across the <q> element, but Internet Explorer doesn't. So, programmers avoid the <q> element. Its value contains a URL that holds additional information regarding the quotation source.

HTML

```
<body>
```

Lorem ipsum dolor sits amet, consectetur adipisicing elit, <q>do eiusmod tempor incididunt ut labore et dolore Magna aliqua</q> Ut enim ad minim veniam,quis nos exercitation ullamco laboris nisi ut aliquip ex ea commodoconsequat.

```
</body>
```

Abbreviation

Utilize the <abbr> element to build abbreviations. The opening tag containing a title attribute is utilized to indicate the full meaning.

HTML

```
<abbr title="International monetary funds">
I.M.F</abbr>
```

Superscript

The <sup> element is utilized to hold superscript characters like the dates suffixes or mathematical methods such as raising a number to a power of 2.

HTML

```
<p>25<sup>th</sup> of October is my birthday</p>
```

Chapter 6:
HTML Lists

There are several reasons to attach a list into your pages. You can create three types of lists in HTML, they are:

Ordered list

Unordered list

Definition list

Ordered list

The HTML <ol> element stands for an ordered list of things, which outputs it in a numbered manner. In an ordered list, you can utilize any of these numbers (1, 2, 3), and alphabets (A, B, C), as well as Roman numerals (i, ii, iii) to set the items on the list.

HTML

<h2>Countries in the world</h2>

<ol>

<li>Australia</li>

<li>Germany</li>

<li>Brazil</li>

<li>United states of America</li>

</ol>

Unordered list

An unordered list is a group of identical items that contain no unique order or succession. The list is built through the use of the HTML <ul> tag. Every list item list is indicated with a bullet. To create a bullet-point list, write the list inside the <ul> element (that means unordered list). Your bullet points should be enclosed within opening <li> and closing </li> tags ("li" means list item).

HTML

<h2> Countries in the world </h2>

<ul>

<li>France</li>

<li>Bolivia</li>

<li>Peru</li>

<li>Azerbaijan</li>

</ul>

Description list

The description list is a unique type of list for terms accompanied by a small text definition or text description. Description lists are enclosed within the <dl> element. The <dl> element also has a <dt> and <dd> description elements within. You will define the <dt> element content. The <dd> element holds the previous <dt> element description.

HTML

```
<dl>
```

```
<dt>Define HTML</dt>
```

```
<dd>
```

Lorem ad minim veniam, quis nostrud exercitation Ipsum dolor sit amet, consectetur adipiscing elit, sed do eiusmod dolore eu fugiat nulla. Ut enimullamco commodo reprehenderit consequat. Duis aute irure dolor in voluptate velit laboris nisi ut aliquip ex ea esse cillum tempor incididunt ut pariaturlabore et dolore Magna aliqua

```
</dd>
```

```
<dt>Define CSS</dt>
```

```
<dd>
```

Lorem ad minim veniam, quis nostrud exercitation Ipsum dolor sit amet, consectetur adipiscing elit, sed do eiusmod dolore eu fugiat nulla. Ut enimullamco commodo reprehenderit consequat. Duis aute irure dolor in voluptate velit laboris nisi ut aliquip ex ea esse cillum tempor incididunt ut pariaturlabore et dolore Magna aliqua

```
</dd>
```

```
<dt>Define Javascript</dt>
```

```
<dd>
```

Lorem ad minim veniam, quis nostrud exercitation Ipsum dolor sit amet, consectetur adipiscing elit, sed do eiusmod dolore eu fugiat nulla. Ut enimullamco commodo reprehenderit consequat. Duis aute irure dolor in voluptate velit laboris nisi ut aliquip ex ea esse cillum tempor incididunt ut pariaturlabore et dolore Magna aliqua

</dd>

</dl>

Nested list

The nested list means a list created inside another list. You can include a sub-list within the <li> element. Web browsers output nested lists in an organized manner a little bit away from the parent list. In a nested unordered list, the browser transforms the list style to bullet point.

HTML

<h2>Countries in the world</h2>

<ul>

    <li>United states of America</li>

    <li>Germany

<ul>

    <li>Spain</li>

    <li>Canada</li>

    <li>Hungary</li>

    <li>Brazil</li>

</ul>

</li>

    <li>Sweden</li>

    <li>France</li>

</ul>

Links

The defining attribute of the web is the link because links enable users to migrate from a web page to another. You can create a list utilizing the <a> element. Contents within the opening <a> and closing </a> can be clicked. You indicate the page you're linking to utilizing the href attribute.

Linking to another site

The anchor tag is used to link in HTML code, the <a> tag. Follow the "a" within the tag with an attribute. If you want to link to other web pages, accompany the "a" with an "href." If you want to link to a separate website, the href attribute value should be the website full web address, you can call that an absolute URL.

By default, Links are shown in blue with an underline by web browsers.

HTML

<a href="http://google.com">Google</a>

Links that open a new tab

Utilize the opening <a> tag target attribute to enable a link open in a new window. _blank should be the attribute value.

HTML

<a href="http://google.com"
target="_blank">Google</a>

Link to other pages on the same site

The opening <a> tag must carry the href attribute.

The href attribute value would be the linked file's name.

HTML

<a href="index.html">Home</a>

Linking to a specific part of the same page

In cases of a long web page, and you want to link to a particular section of that page to avoid scrolling up and down the page to locate that section. The destination anchor permits the author to indicate particular points within a page that a source anchor point. Example of linking to a particular page section on web pages include:

"Back to top" – this is often under a long page.

HTML

<body>

<h2>Linking and Navigation</h2>

    <p>This page explains the following languages</p>

<ul>

    <li><a href="#html">Define Html</a></li>

    <li><a href="#CSS">Define CSS</a></li>

    <li><a href="#JavaScript">Define JavaScript</a></li>

</ul>

<h3 id="html">Define Html</h3>

    <p>Lorem ad minim veniam, quis nostrud exercitation Ipsum dolor sit amet, consectetur adipiscing elit, sed do eiusmod dolore eu fugiat nulla.

Ut enimullamco commodo reprehenderit consequat. Duis aute irure dolor in voluptate velit laboris nisi ut aliquip ex ea esse cillum tempor incididunt ut pariaturlabore et dolore Magna aliqua   </p>

                        <a href="#top">back to top</a>

<h3 id="CSS">Define CSS</h3>

    <p>Lorem ad minim veniam, quis nostrud exercitation Ipsum dolor sit amet, consectetur adipiscing elit, sed do eiusmod dolore eu fugiat nulla. Ut enimullamco commodo reprehenderit consequat. Duis aute irure dolor in voluptate velit laboris nisi ut aliquip ex ea esse cillum tempor incididunt ut pariaturlabore et dolore Magna aliqua   </p>

                        <a href="#top">back to top</a>

<h3 id="JavaScript">Define JavaScript</h3>

    <p>Lorem ad minim veniam, quis nostrud exercitation Ipsum dolor sit amet, consectetur adipiscing elit, sed do eiusmod dolore eu fugiat nulla. Ut enimullamco commodo reprehenderit consequat. Duis aute irure dolor in voluptate velit laboris nisi ut aliquip ex ea esse cillum tempor incididunt ut pariaturlabore et dolore Magna aliqua </p>

<a href="#top">back to top</a>

</body>

Link to a particular part of another page

Linking to a particular section of a separate page is easy to accomplish. Make sure the page you are linking to contains id attributes that specify the particular section of the page. You can attach the syntax to the end of that page link. So, the href attribute will hold the page address (absolute or relative URL), accompanied by the # syntax, and then utilize the id attribute value on the linking element. For instance, the code is written like this: <a href="http:/www.htmlandcssbook.com#bottom">\

Links to other files (ZIP files, Word documents, PDFs, etc.)

Place a link on items such as images and pdf drives and not just text. If you want to share PDF file with others, write the code would like this:

HTML

<a href="html.docx">Download my CV</a>

Chapter 7:
What is Coding

Just as the saying goes, coding runs the world. Although a whole lot of people do not realize it exists or what it even means. The first act of writing in a programming language is called coding. Let me take you through a little process. Launch your web browser and right click on any part of your browser window, and click View Page Source. Now ask yourself, do you understand what you see? They are written codes mostly written in HTML programming language with bits of CSS and JavaScript. Coding is a script that the computer understands. The script can command the computer to do your bidding if your code right.

Your computer does not understand your chain of codes at all. The machine only understands Yes and No or Binary codes (1 and 0). The programming language that you write only tells the computer what to do. The computer speaks Binary, but understands several programming languages just like you know programming and your native language.

Why You Should Learn Coding

Coding can have a massive influence on your professional and life. Below are a few reasons why you should learn and understand coding.

Coding hugely increases your potential earnings.

Professional programmers and coders charge high hourly rates. A lot of professional coders will reject hourly rate short of $100 per hour, which is a fantastic income. The best part of it is that there is a scarcity of coders, which means extra profit.

Coding lets you work for yourself. Although there are lots of coders working on more significant contract's at large companies all around the world, you can also work in freelance roles. Being a freelance coder, and it gives you the capacity to choose where to work and when and how you want to.

You work on your projects. Being a coder gives you the ability to develop websites and you're really only limited by your imagination.

Types of Coders

You need to understand that there are several types of coders, and each one focuses on separate things. Coders can become game developers, systems engineers, and AI programmers, etc.

Front-End Developer

Front-end developers are website builders. They handle the layout, design, and appearance on a webpage through the use of front-end languages like CSS, JavaScript, and HTML.

A few functions of front-end web developers are writing the code layout of a design and transforming it into a website. They create functional and interactive websites. It includes things like building hyperlinked buttons, placing animations, etc.

Back-End Developer

The back-end developer develops web apps that run the website. Web apps are designed to perform a particular task.

A few functions of back-end web developers are the creation of an account on a website, logging in and out of a website, building profiles, and connecting with friends on social media.

Chapter 8:
Introduction to
Raspberry Pi

The Raspberry Pi is a sequence of little single-board computers built in the United Kingdom. Raspberry Pi Foundation established Raspberry Pi to enhance the knowledge of computer science basics in institutions and developed countries. The authentic Raspberry Pi model became more popular than expected. It sold above its expected target for uses like robotics without peripherals (keyboards and mice). A few accessories are available in various bundles (official and unofficial).

The Ingredients for a Raspberry Pi 2

USB ports

The Raspberry Pi 2 contains four USB ports, and it lets you attach it to mice, keyboards, USB sticks and WiFi dongles holding all of your documents. The ports do not supply a lot of power; therefore, if you would attach a USB hub to the Pi, find the one with an additional power supply.

Ethernet port

The old way to get an internet connection is through a

wire named Ethernet cable. Locate these ports at the router's rear which allows you attach the Raspberry Pi to it directly. This concept is set up quickly, unlike WiFi, and supplies better internet, but it is limited by the cable length.

GPIO header

It contains the all-purpose input/output (GPIO) pins. GPIO pins are a group of connections with several functions, but their primary function lets you attach the Raspberry Pi to an electronic circuit. Then you can program the Pi to influence the circuit and perform beautiful things with it.

Audio out

It looks similar to a headphone socket, a 3.5mm jack precisely, this enables the connection of the Pi to the device speakers, or your headphones and contain a Raspberry jam.

MicroSD card slot

Utilize a small SD card as the hard drive of the Raspberry Pi. Many systems cannot be attached directly to a microSD card; therefore, you will need an adaptor that goes into the SD card slots.

Power

It is the small charging port within your smartphone. It is a micro-USB port, and it means that the Pi can be powered with the right phone charger or through the PC. It is advisable to utilize the official Raspberry Pi power supply to ensure the Pi gets the right amount of power.

HDMI port

It is the kind of port located at the back of modern televisions as well as the monitors of computers. Utilize HDMI cable to attach the Raspberry Pi to the screen to watch what it does.

Configuration Tool Tabs

There are four tabs in the Raspberry Pi Configuration. They let you develop several parts of your Pi.

System

With the system, you can fix the Pi boots to the command line (CLI), create autologin, and alter the password. It also contains an overscan setting that helps eradicate the black border across the desktop if one exists.

Interfaces

Several interfaces on the Raspberry Pi can be allowed or disallowed below this tab, which includes camera and connectors.

Performance

You can develop GPU memory allocation to enhance performance to execute a specific operation.

Localization

This tab lets you develop the right language, keyboard layout, and time zone.

Software Configuration Tool

When Raspbian has loaded and displays on the

desktop, select Menu to launch the main menu. Choose the Preferences option and tool Configuration on the submenu. It creates a tool that is utilized to configure several options on the Raspberry Pi. Note that the essential choice to change is the Expand Filesystem option. Raspbian does not need a lot of space to run, so you should tell it to utilize every available space on the SD card to store files if you want it that way. So, select the Expand Filesystem on the Pi Configuration menu, and reload the Pi when prompted. Select Shutdown, and choose Reboot, then tap OK.

Set Up Your Raspberry Pi

Download NOOBS

There are lots of operating systems that comes with the Raspberry Pi that you can utilize. You can install them manually. Although there is an easy way to install the OSes, which is through the NOOBS or Out of Box Software. It contains every new version of the Raspberry Pi operating system. Utilize NOOBS full version because it includes Raspbian already, which makes the operation slightly faster rather than NOOBS Lite.

Install SD Card

Get the SD card ready to function correctly on the Raspberry Pi. Remove every vital documents or information because you will have to format the SD card. Install the SD Card Formatter 4.0 instrument to get the card ready. Format the SD card and remove the files within the NOOBS zip folder then place them on the card. Now NOOBS prepared to be used on the SD card.

Connect the Cables

Remove the SD card adaptor, extract the microSD card, then place it in the Raspberry Pi. Plug an HDMI cable in between the screen and the Raspberry Pi, the router's Ethernet cable (or USB WIFI dongle), together with a keyboard and mouse. Then connect the power cable to Raspberry Pi.

Install Raspbian

When the Raspberry Pi turns on, it will show few screen texts, disregard it until it reaches a menu that lists every operating system. It lets you choose several OSes at a go, but right, we will focus on Raspbian. Choose Raspbian, select Install, and the installation operation begins, which could take some time to finish execution.

Installing and Updating Software

Install New Software

When you install the Raspbian, it gives you access to a lot of several programs. Raspbian can be installed through the use of terminal because Raspbian has no app store. Utilize the below command to find the Raspbian on the terminal:

$ apt-cache search FTP

It sends back packages with details. Utilize the package name to install any of the software, but for us, FileZilla returns as FTP client. FileZilla is the package name. To install, we use:

sudo apt-get install FileZilla

The above will download the package and all required software needed to run the package, then install to Raspbian.

Update Your Software and OS

Raspbian software periodically updates online, and it fixes security updates and bugs. They do not sync automatically with Raspberry Pi; always check for updates on your system. The terminal handles this operation similar to software installation. The update process is of two parts: firstly, update repositories (list of software and versions available on your system). Achieve that by inputting the command:

sudo apt-get update

It checks online to see the software repositories state and gives result to Raspberry Pi, and it will save changes. It then decides which software to be updated, but instruct it to execute the update with the following command:

sudo apt-get upgrade

The Raspbian operating system may require a significant or massive update or significant changes like a browser or new interface, etc. It doesn't happen regularly, but when it occurs, execute the upgrade with:

sudo apt dist-upgrade

Chapter 9:
Introduction to Black-Hat Hacking

The word "hacker" alone has amassed a lot of negative feelings. Traits like breaking into devices and stealing sensitive and private information are usually what you hear about hackers. A large population of the world's computer users has gone through the effects of hacking activities which includes spyware attacks, virus attacks, and various types of malware that penetrate, slow down, or damage your device. Anyway, it is not every hacker that is deceitful and untrustworthy, who offer nothing other than privacy violations. The word "hacker" has a good and useful meaning. Traditionally, a hacker is a person who enjoys attempting to improve computers and other electronics. They get to know everything about the computer system and functions and then do the work to search for ways to improve them. In other words, hackers are the people to turn to when it comes to enhancing your computers and making your device function better and faster. But in today's world, a black-hat hacker is a person that obtains electronic information without permission, by dubious gains, and for self interest. Although many ethical hackers exist, they are white-hat hackers, while the suspicious and corrupt hackers are called the black-hat hackers.

To apprehend a hacker, you need another hacker to do the job and catch the hacker, and to your advantage, there are lots of ethical hackers who are willing to get the job done. Hacking is also a computer skill that you can use both ways, good or bad.

Objectives of Hacking

The world's perception today about hackers is the black-hat hacker's way, the act of obtaining vital information dubiously. Ethical hacking is utilized to discover your device or network weak points and get them secured so the black hats do not have access to transform or manipulate and use your information against you. The motive of white-hat hackers is to run security checks, fix all loopholes, and ensure information and device security. The white hat section has adopted a different name, and they call themselves penetration testing specialists. One rule that helps you to differentiate between penetration testing and dubious hackers is that the white-hat hackers get the permission of device owners before they breach their security. During that operation, when the penetration testing completes, the device owner receives a very secure network or device system. When the entire penetration testing process ends, the hacker then recommends few security solutions and how to fix problems.

The Caveat

One thing you cannot expect is to have everything protected. The idea of totally securing any device, computer, or electronic system from potential attacks is farfetched. You can achieve that only by unplugging the device from all possible networks and keeping it safe far from all contacts. That renders the contained information useless to everyone. In the hacking world, it is tough to plan for anything because there are a lot of unknowns in this incredibly connected game. You should also know that the next time you turn on your WiFi and allow your friends to connect, you have just created a way for hackers to get in. Let's talk about some general security liabilities black-hat hackers relate with and monitor closely.

Network Infrastructure Attacks

Network infrastructure attacks can bypass and get into local networks and on the Internet. Too many systems are accessible through the internet, which makes it very easy to break. You can hack into a system by attaching a modem to the local network. Another concept of a network intrusion is through NetBIOS, TCP/IP, and several transport mechanisms inside a network. Other tricks are building denial services by sending a massive number of requests. You can use network analyzers to get data packets that move across the web. They examine the data they get and disclose the information they contain. Another trick is when WiFi networks are not protected. You must have heard too many stories of people moving around with tablets, laptops, or smartphones searching for unprotected WiFi signal to manipulate.

Non-Technical Attacks

This type of attack involves tricking people into

disclosing their passwords, willingly or not. It is similar to social engineering, and that is the exact tool utilized for these types of attacks. One example is paying, duping, or bribing a colleague to disclose usernames and passwords. Another concept of non-technical hack is other people's computer room, load the system, and then extract every piece of needed information. Yes, it sounds like the most comfortable thing on earth. In reality, non-technical hacks are an integral part of the hacking tactics.

Attacks on an Operating System

The operating system attacks are regularly performed hacks. There are a lot of computers out there without any protection. Therefore, there are various loopholes in a lot of operating systems. Even the newest ones contain a few bugs that hackers can manipulate. One of the ways to hack the operating system is through hacking the password or attacking the encryption mechanisms.

Attacks on Applications

Online applications that use internet connectivity get thousands of attacks (web applications and email server software applications). One attack type is spam mail, which goes back as far as the year 2000. Spam mail contains a lot of things that can break into your device. You can also utilize malware or harmful software to attack a lot of things, and the primary target is apps. Software programs like worms, trojan horses, spyware, and viruses. These programs can access your device online. Another type of applications attacked regularly is Simple Mail Transfer Protocols applications (SMTP) and Hypertext Transfer Protocols applications (HTTP). A lot of these apps bypass firewalls of computer users automatically. You should know all these tricks to provide excellent protection to your computer system from a powerful attack.

Hacking Basics

This section explains some essential hacking tools and techniques. These tools are available in several hacking methods. These are the most straightforward form of black-hat hacking you can learn.

Social Engineering

A non-technical hack is called social engineering. It means using the regularly used available resources to users and companies. When it comes to companies, the company's employees are the target. People put their trust in other people by nature. It is a loophole for hackers to manipulate any organization. They only need to get the details from one person, and then they can utilize those details to obtain additional information from another coworker, and the trend continues. For example, a computer hacker could pose as a computer repair or tech support rep and approach a particular company. They often tell companies employees to download a few free software or subscribe to a service that they can manipulate easily. Sometimes a black-hat hacker boldly asks for the company username and password. Phishing sites also offer the same services. These websites are created to collate information. Some sites contain several similar visual layouts or patterns like the original site. They trick customers of a particular website into signing into a lookalike website. These websites then collate the customers' passwords and usernames. Black-hat hackers can obtain PayPal logins, credit card information, and several important pieces of information. With social engineering concept of hacking, you only need to look official and professional to a total stranger.

Social Engineering Basic Steps

The first thing to do is to collate data about a particular company or personnel. Hackers perform these research themselves. Then, they utilize the information with finance organizations, the SEC, and every bit of valuable information. The larger the company, the more you can obtain information about it. Hackers find their way into the company's trash to get information. A lot of employees dump a lot of enticing documents such as printed emails, meeting notes, network diagrams, organizational charts, and several lists of employee's phone numbers into the trash can. The black-hat hackers build trust. They contact customers or employees utilizing obtained information. They pretend to be one of the company's personnel and acts nicely and ready to be of help. Hackers communicate victims through chat, emails, or voicemail to look official and professional.

Countermeasures to Social Engineering

The best way to counter social engineering concept of

hacking is to ensure you notify the public. Ensure your employees and customers are up to date of your official communication protocol and to be cautious of anybody who demands login information or any valuable information.

Compromising Physical Security Flaws

One significant part of information security is the physical security. Physical security hackers can bypass and break into their computers. They cannot avoid the company's firewall but can attach a hardware or software component in your network within your firewall by coming into your computer room and attach a tool into one employee's device. Some hackers want more than connecting a tool and bypass your security from within, and some would access and steal vital information. They can sneak into your organization through the employee smoking areas, cafeteria doors, or any available entry point.

Hacking Passwords

Password hacking is one of the hackers' favorites. It can be achieved using social engineering and endangering physical liabilities within the workplace. One way to hack another person's password is to spy on them when they input it on a device. Password hacking is one usual way for hackers to obtain data through a computer network. Another method, called inference, enables hackers to collate as much data of an employee such as birthdates, children names, favorite things, phone numbers, favorite TV shows, and others. Hackers use these when trying to guess your password. There are several top-notch tech ways to guess other people's password. The tools to hack a password include a few remote cracking services, network analyzers, and several types of software to crack a password. You probably must have heard about application programs using brute force. It is a trial-and-error concept of password guessing. Brute force tries every possible combination to achieve the password. It takes time before they acquire the password. It is a crucial exhaustive search concept. Many hackers focus on physical flaws and break into people's computer to find their passwords. Microsoft operating systems often save passwords within the same directory called the security accounts manager (SAM). Sometimes the operating system saves passwords inside an existing database file, such as ntds.dit as an example. Users develop emergency repair disks within a USB drive. What you need to do is access the directory (for example, c:\winnt\repair). You can find passwords within the system's registry. Some employees also store passwords in text files, which is easy for hackers to obtain. Another method is to install keyloggers. They can be bits of software or hardware which logs the keystrokes of unaware users. There are a lot of keystroke logging software programs that you can buy, and some are even free.

Network Hacking

Hacking a network is an operation of too many forms. One instance is when people break into other people's internet or WiFi connection to browse for free. Within a network, make sure you scan the network to search for unprotected connected network device connected. Now access the data. One instance for that is the moment you are logged to a WiFi network, launch your windows explorer and select Network. Then check the file sharing and network discovery. If it is within that specific network, search for a connected device to access the documents within it.

War Dialing

If you intend to understand the old ways of breaking into other people's network, then war dialing is your target and will fulfill your desires. This concept of hacking utilizes the advantage of liabilities in other people's telephone system. The idea requires the use of war dialing software. Hackers can identify repeat dial tones and password inputs at the dial tone and place calls to any locations freely. Hackers can access voicemail for phone systems utilizing PBX switches.

Network Structure Vulnerabilities

You can find vulnerabilities on every computer network. No matter how small the weaknesses are, hackers can always exploit it. The utensils required for network hacking is the same tools necessary to identify defects within your network. Devices such as network scanners, DNS lookups, and require network queries.

Few scanners can perform ping sweeps and port scanning. Other scanners can also perform SMTP relay testing. You require a scanner that performs host port probing and operating system fingerprinting as well as testing firewalls. Port scanners can list the devices on your network. Port scanners are easy to utilize, and you can test any device with one. Every regular hacked port utilizes the TCP protocols but while some utilize UDP. The regular ports and services related to them are 23 (Telnet), 22 (SSH), 7 (Echo), 53 (DNS), 21 (FTP control), 80 (HTTP), 25 (SMTP), 443 (HTTPS), 19 (Chargen), 1433 (Microsoft SQL Server), and 20 (FTP data) and so on.

Breaking into WiFi Networks

Wireless networks used at home, cafes, offices, or anywhere are all vulnerable to hacking. Gone are those days that open WiFi networks are secured. It means that you can hack any connected device to the internet through wireless. Hackers only need to find free public networks. Anybody can get online and break into your internet. The only safeguard measure for people against hackers is the signal range from the WiFi router. Those were the days of signal amplifiers and antennas. The only available security to WiFi router users was Wireless Encryption Protocol (WEP). Although with this, hackers can monitor you and will crack your WEP code because the design is poor. Nowadays, there is no need for WiFi signal limits. A lot of routers consist of 1,500 feet range, about 500 meters. The only difference from the old ways is that new routers utilize WiFi Protected Access (WPA) and WPA2 (WIFI Protected Access 2) to be their security protocols type, and they are better than WEP. To hack into your friend's WiFi connection, make sure you monitor the WiFi activity and grab the data when they log their device onto the access point or router. It looks like a difficult task, but there is a way to go around it. You only need to dispatch a death frame. They are packets which you will transfer to the access point like the wireless router that disconnects all other connected devices to that particular network. They will have to log in again, then you can apprehend the login data itself.

Tools for Hacking into Wireless Connections

There are lots of wireless connections hacking tools available today. There is a payment attached to get premium quality of some while there is also some open-source (free) ones which will perform decently. Search and download the penetration testing software (Aircrackng and so on). Wireless penetration programs can apprehend pcap (packet capture) files. Apprehending takes about one hour. Now ask yourself, what do I do with this packet capture files? Some penetration testing software evaluates the information for you. However, if you are using a free penetration testing software and functionality is limited, then another tool is needed to crack the packet capture files. These tools are called password crackers. There are few free password crackers while others come at a price. You need to install some on your device while the rest are online applications. The primary operation of the password crackers tool is to check the packet capture files against a database that contains millions of passwords. Sometimes it takes minutes or even seconds to crack passwords with these tools. Cracking software often breaks the PIN into several equal halves. The pin contains eight characters. You need to understand that the pin last character of that pin is only a checksum. It means that the first seven are only digits/characters that would crack. Make sure you do not transmit its SSID, which is the assigned name to the wireless network by the user. Few routers contain MAC filtering that permits only listed computers to gain entry the wireless network. The apprehended MAC addresses can be copied and used as your own. That process is called spoofing.

Hacking Your Own Windows Password

A lot of people have this habit of forgetting passwords, and this occurs each day. So, what happens when anyone or even you can forget your password and cannot log into your personal computer. It is one kind of situation that you are going to enjoy your hacking skills. However, it is essential to know that hacking into people's computers is illegal, and you can only do that when you are paid to do the job.

Default Administrator Account

Let's assume that you possess a machine running on Windows 7. One of the ways to achieve your goal is to utilize the default Windows 7 Administrator account. It is often disabled when you launch the device in normal mode. So, reload the machine in Safe Mode. Then choose default administrator on Windows 7. The default administrator requires no password. When you get to that stage, leave the password box blank and click log in. When you are in, you can head to the Control panel and modify the password giving you troubles.

Password Reset Disk

This disk can also be called the password reset file. It has a little wizard program which guides users to develop new passwords for Windows user account that you forgot the password. Develop this disk when you install the operating system. Attach the plug to the device and select Reset Password. Now follow the prompts. It will demand to know where it can find the reset password files, so choose the right drive. The prompt will tell you to create a new password. Now follow the prompt instructions.

What Does This Book Have to Offer?

I have divided this book into seven chapters to offer you step-by-step learning of each language. This offers you an opportunity to jump to the chapter that you want to start first. However, it is recommended that you start from Chapter 1 in order to get a feel of how a programmer thinks and how a website is built. You can move on from simple to complex. Let's see what you will get to know in different sections of this book.

The first section of this book tells you about the benefits of the languages which you are going to learn. You will understand the benefits of learning each programming language, and how can you use this knowledge to have financial benefits in the world markets. Also, you will know how each language is a building block for a full website development experience.

The second section is about learning HTML which is the basis for developing a website from scratch. You will learn about creating lists, tables, forms, texts and other structures on a webpage. When you reach the end of the section, you will already have created a webpage on the back of the code I have given in the book. It is recommended that you edit the code and create your own to learn it better.

The third section of this book is about Java. The section will educate you on the package files in Java and different types of primitive and non-primitive data in Java. In addition, you will learn about Java strings, object orientation, classes, and the class variable. This chapter ends with the conditional statements in Java. The idea behind writing this chapter is to show you how Java works at the basic level.

The fourth section is on C++ programming language. You will be able to understand the basic structure of C++ and computation. In addition, you will learn about strings and loops which form the basics of C++ programming. At the end of the chapter, comes functions. At the beginner level, this chapter offers plenty of coding to get the feel on how to do programming in C++ language.

The fifth section of this book will offer you a comprehensive understanding of Structured Query Language (SQL), which is about the creation, manipulation, and management of huge databases. The chapter offers you to learn the basics of table creation in SQL. After that, you will find practical examples of managing a real database. When you have gone through the entire chapter, you will be able to prepare reports at your office by retrieving different data records and printing them out. You will have a solid base in SQL, which will help you take a higher flight for professional learning and usage.

The second-to-last section of the book is about programming in Python. Just like all the other languages, you will learn the basics of Python like its structure, codes, commands, creating lists, decoding lists, and a lot about Python dictionaries.

The last section of the book will walk you further into the world of Python. You will learn about functions, classes, and creation of objects in Python. It will educate you on how sensitive Python is when it comes to little things such as quotation marks. You will learn about escape characters that kill Python's sensitivity to different characters.

Prerequisites to reading this book

I don't expect you to be a programmer for reading and understanding this book. I only expect you to keep your attention intact. That's enough! Anyone can read this book and understand the world of these five languages.

First of all, it is necessary that you have a functional computer by your side with standard specifications to load different types of software like the Python shell, C++ compiler, Notepad++, and MySQL command prompt. When you have set up the system, you are ready to start reading this book and practicing the code. Make it a step-by-step learning process. Learn one code or statement by heart and run it on the compiler or command prompt. Keep learning new codes and testing them to see what each snippet of code brings to you.

Chapter 10:
Usage of Various
Programming Languages

In the 1990s, when users browsed through a website, they confronted dry, plain, and somewhat static web pages. We have come a long way since then. Now, you enjoy dynamic web content when you enter a URL address in a browser or search it out through Google or Bing. If you are a frequent visitor of a website, its content will shape itself overtime according to your interests and choices.

Website owners create dynamic content to offer their visitors customized experience and quality time while they stay on your website. It is a face that there is no shortage of websites that still contain static content. This does undue damage to their reputation in the open markets when their competitors, after realizing the importance of dynamic website content, outsmart them by investing in a complete overhaul of their websites to make their highly interactive.

Top businesses consider their websites as an asset to amplify marketing range of their products and services. Some businesses have leaped across seas to reach other continents and to give a major boost to their business. If you own a Mercedez showroom and you want to increase your reach across the continents, you are in need of a dynamic website. As a user I would like to see a 360-degree view of a car that you have put on sale. I would like to view its tires, the central console, the backseats, the front, the back and the dashboard. If your website allows me to spin the car, this would be the best, for sure. As a buyer, I would like to be able to explore the details of the car. If those details are packed into headings that would unleash a pop up list of details upon navigation of the cursor, I would highly appreciate it as it would be fast and easy to explore the details about different parts of the car.

In addition, it will add to the credibility of your business. As a car business owner, I expect you to put on an interactive quotation form on the website, in which I would enter my price range and get a list of available cars in your showroom or I would enter the specifications of the car that I want and the program returns the result if it matches a car in your showroom. This would be perfect. I would more likely to buy a car from a showroom which has set up such as tremendous website for their customers.

You can add a blog which you will have to update with the latest news about cars, engine oil, maintenance, and new car technology. This will portray you as a generous seller and help you pull in more customers. In addition to a regularly updated blog, you need to connect your website with your social media accounts such as Facebook, Twitter and LinkedIn. Your website should have videos, ebooks, whitepapers. If you want your visitors to have a more dynamic experience, you can add graphics and media (Hanson, 2018).

Benefits of learning HTML

HTML is comparatively easy to learn. Even understanding the code is not that much difficult. Dubbed as the foundation of web development, HTML has simple tags that are the basis of its structure. Each tag has a specific value and each tag serves a special purpose. If you happen to read the HTML code of a website, you can easily understand the basic job of each tag in that particular code. As opposed to other programming languages, HTML doesn't return an error code. It will build the parts of the code that has the right tags and only show faulty display in that particular section which carries the mistake. You can say that it is somewhat less frustrating than other languages.

Almost all the web browsers support the HTML code. Furthermore, it is considered as the most SEO-friendly language. Search engines can easily read it and rank it at a higher level in the search results that's why it is the top choice of web developers and designers. It achieves this by a reduced parsing time and a super-fast page loading time.

When it comes to web development, the important thing is editing the language you are using. Websites are dynamic and they need to be updated in content, structure and design, that's why you need to build a website with a language that can be edited more often and efficiently. HTML is one of those languages which offers easy editing. All you need a text editor like Notepad in the Windows operating system. You can also download its latest version, the Notepad++ for colorful coding to better read and understand the tags. Simply by opening the file in a text editor, you can start editing right away.

Apart from all these benefits, another one is that you can easily integrate HTML with other languages like PHP, JAVASCRIPT, and CSS. You also can change the display of HTML in the blink of an eye. Open the editor, change the code, save it and then open it on a browser. You can see the changes you have made instantly on the browser. This makes HTML the favorite of web developers (Advantages of HTML, n.d).

Benefits of learning Java

Java has considerable benefits over other programming languages due to the fact that it offers portability to programmers. You can pick up a program and transport it to any other computer system or mobile phone as Java operates independent of the platform on which it is being compiled. You can run it on any computer system that a JVM installed on it. Java has been regularly used and updated which makes it reliable and free of any dysfunctionalities, unpredictability, and instability. The user community, additionally, is huge in Java which makes it easier to learn and understand as you can source codes, programs and discuss the errors you get returned in the compiler.

Java is considered as a high-level programming language which was initially created to run set-top boxes. It was not before 1995 that Java caught the eye of web developers across the world. Still, programmers are using it for mobile applications because it is very simple to compile and debug. The automatic memory allocation feature of Java makes it a fun thing for programmers.

Java has object-oriented feature which allows you to create reusable code for the ease of programmers. In addition, programmers can create different objects in the classes and get them interacted among multiple objects.

Java is considered one of the most secure languages in the world of programming. The security feature is integrated in the design of the language. The creators of Java developed each item in this language with the security feature in mind. We can understand this by checking the Java Virtual Machine which verifies the bytecode before running it. Java also offers programmers to multithread their operations.

Benefits of learning C++

Generally, a C++ program consists of different commands which guide the computer into acting in a certain way or finish a certain task. C++ is considered a portable language, and it can be exported to other computer systems. It is highly beneficial for multiplatform app development. C++ retains features of both low-level as well as high-level programming languages.

C++ is attractive for programmers due to the fact that it is an object-oriented language, and it includes some complex concepts like data abstraction, classes, and encapsulation. C++ allows programmers to reuse the code, which is easy and facilitating. They are saved from the frustration of repeat writing the code again and again as the need arises. In addition, the multiparadigm programming feature of C++ is a huge plus as programmers get to have three different paradigms like objected-oriented programs, generic programs, and imperative programs.

If you want to create a program at a low-level like creating a program for calculation at a superstore, C++ provides a handy tool which yields the best result while offering simplicity and time-efficiency for the programmer and the user.

C++ also offers programmers a wide range of app development features. You can create games, do arithmetic and also create applications for graphical user interface (GUI). In addition, it is scalable. It also is static, and you have to type-check before running a program, which makes it more efficient as programmers make it a habit to double check the code before they execute it on a compiler.

C++ is great for creating some complex programs because it has a huge community size, which offers programmers great support if they happen to get stuck somewhere in the middle of writing a code.

Last, but not least, is the job circle of C++ programmers. C++ is used in virtual reality, development of games and mobile apps, and also in some complex industries like finance (Varma, 2018).

Benefits of learning SQL

Structured Query Language (SQL) is one of the most amazing in the world of programming. It has revolutionized the way data are handled across the world. It has enabled big firms, finance companies, and industries to store huge files of data in a general database. A remarkable thing about SQL is also the speed and efficiency by which it stores and processes data. A trained user takes a few seconds to retrieve bundles of information from the database to create reports for their boss and other company executives like the board members.

SQL is easy to use because a layman, who has no knowledge of coding, can easily use it and manage the entire database system. Although a little amount of coding is needed for the management, users can learn it in a short time.

You can use SQL in your laptop, personal computer, or even on your cell phones. This portability of SQL makes it the hot favorite in the corporate sector where employees are supposed to work on their PCs, cell phones, and laptops, all at the same time.

In addition to that, SQL is a highly interactive language. You can interact directly with the database by pushing forward your questions about a certain piece of information and receiving answers. It saves lots of time for a business. You can perform a number of operations on the database that has been stored on the computer system.

Its open source makes it one of the most-loved languages for database management. Some databases from MySQL are free or are very cost-efficient when it comes to operations.

If you are newly handed over the task to manage a SQL database at your office, you can learn it in no time because it generally consists of statements in English which makes it easy to understand. SQL offers programmers an easy way to fix databases in web and mobile applications. Nowadays, demand for SQL databases is rising because new businesses are getting online fast, and they need web apps with SQL databases in order to safely and efficiently store customer data.

It is a complete package. You can create a full-fledged database and then maintain its security. You also can update old databases in addition to sharing them with your users. SQL offers a wide range of databases that can be viewed from a number of angles. SQL can also serve as a language which connects the user to the server. Your customers can directly store their data in the database just by entering it on the front-end of your website.

As a job seeker, you should be glad to hear that SQL is an in-demand skill. There is no shortage of IT offices, banks, retail businesses. and web development companies which area always seeking SQL experts (12 Benefits of SQL (Structured Query Language), n.d).

If a business doesn't understand its data, it cannot succeed even in the long run. It is imperative for corporations and retail businesses to analyze the customers' data in order to understand the buying patterns, the average buying capacity of their customers, the average products which remained hot in demand. You also need to know which product sold more in which season. This information can be found stored in your SQL database. You can retrieve it anytime and run an analysis for drafting a business policy or revising an existing one to give a major boost to your business. Data analysis is essential for your business to remain in the competition. You can get to know the following things after an analysis of SQL database.

- You know which social group your customers generally belong to?
- What is their buying power?
- What products they like the most?
- Which season remains hot with respect to customer visits?
- Which products are going obsolete?
- Which special occasions attract most of the buyers?

If you have a business, which has fulfilled all the conditions for being successful in the market, but still it is not thriving, you probably are the victim of ignorance: the ignorance of sifting through databases and receiving pearls of wisdom from their galleries.mSQL provides an easy way to conduct your research, do your analysis, and take decisive action.

Benefits of learning Python

Python has come a long way to be what it is today. Python is popular among programmers because it has lots of implementations. Let's take a look at some of them.

- Enterprise as well as web applications
- Development of games
- Prototyping
- Processing of images as well as other graphic design applications
- Web applications
- Operating systems
- Computational applications

Python has a great number of support libraries in which you can find string operations, OS interfaces, tools for web service, and other related things. You can find a great number of programming tasks in a scripted state to be used as per your needs. Programmers save time and effort by using programs from these libraries. There are third-party modules in Python that allow programmers to interact with other computer languages.

Another advantage of Python is that it's open source, which is free for the learning purpose as well as commercial use. Python is also quite easy to learn when compared with the other programming languages. It is very easy to read and has a simple syntax which turns out to be very helpful for beginners. You can consult from PEP 8, the Python style guide, if you are stuck somewhere in the middle of formatting a code. The style guide is easy to comprehend. If you are at an advanced stage of formatting a code for a program and need an entire program to include in your code, you can quite possibly get it from a vibrant user community that has been recharging the internet resource of Python on a continuous basis.

Python is object-oriented hence it provides its users amazing control ability. You can create an object and automate it to conduct certain tasks (Rongola, 2015).

Chapter 11:
Introduction to HTML

The world of website development is changing fast, but HTML is not going anywhere anytime soon. HTML can be dubbed as the foundation block of a web page. This text-based markup language is very easy to learn for anyone with a non-technical background. I can safely bet that out of the multi-billion web pages, each page contains at least some HTML. It defines the content. I'll try to get you acquainted with how HTML works and how you can use it to build your own web pages.

When HTML originated in the 1990s, it merely consisted of paragraphing techniques, creating headings, forming lists and interlinking different web pages. As time went by, many new elements were consistently added to HTML, which transformed its outlook. HTML is often taught and discussed in combination with CSS. In simple words, HTML is the skeleton of a web page while CSS is the skin. What a web page contains and how it performs are the two jobs of HTML, and how it looks is what CSS is for. The latter adds colors and a variety of graphics to the web page to make appear cool and eye-catching.

When I was in the phase of learning computer languages, I was lucky to have a teacher named Abby. She was wonderful in coding, swimming, cycling, and of course, teaching. I learnt so much from her in a short time. Abby was a proud owner of dogs. When I was an aspiring student of computer languages, Abby and I used to walk her dogs to parks and lake sides. Such a lovely time to remember! Abby explained once the connection between HTML and CSS, and it was genius. If you draw a table in HTML code and want to make it easily readable and colorful, you have to invoke CSS. So, HTML produces the raw material while CSS makes value added products. Let's move on to learn some HTML coding.

The Structure and The Text

Everything in the world has to follow a structure to be efficient and precise. For example, a cellular service a set structure to process text messages. Nowadays, almost everything like newspapers, telephone directories, and shopping have gone online. All these websites are built on a basic structure for proper functioning. If you are an avid magazine reader, you might have taken time to analyze the basic structure of a featured articles. It has a main heading, a tagline, multiple subheadings, tables, graphs, and information in the form of lists with bullet points or numbers.

If you care about the aesthetics of your web page and you want people to scan it easily, you need to build it in a proper structure. For that purpose, you can use HTML coding to enclose the text that you want to appear before the visitors of your website. The code can be added through an editor, such as Notepad, just like the following.

```html
<html>
<head>
<title>Elon Left a Tesla Stroller in Space</title>
</head>
<body>
<h1>The Falcon Heavy returned home safely.</h1>
<p>Elon blasted off a Tesla on a Falcon heavy that dislodged it out in the wilds of space just above the earth's atmosphere. The pictures that the Tesla sent back were amazing stuff. It was incredible to see a rocket landing back on Earth quite intact after traveling thousands of kilometers. Elon must be proud of his team.</p>
<h2>The Falcon Heavy landed exactly on the launching pad from which it took off.</h2>
<p>This made another headline for 24 hours as the Falcon Heavy landed on the same launch pad from which it took off.</p>
<h3>Mission accomplished</h3>
<p>Elon had a dream to make reusable rockets which he has quite successfully achieved.</p>
</body>
</html>
```

You can easily differentiate between the HTML code that is inside angle brackets and the content on the webpage. There are h2 and h3 headings and paragraphs in the content for better reading. The angled brackets carry information and directions for the browser which reads the code and displays the text accordingly. The angled brackets are also known as HTML tags or simply the tags. One notable thing to remember is the closing tag that has a forward slash. Don't forget to insert the slash to close the tag or the code won't work as expected. That's what Abby taught me in the very first lesson. Please note that there is a head of the page that contains title. A browser reads this section as the title of the web page and displays it either on the top of the web page or in the URL itself. You can a code similar to the above written in an editor, such as Notepad++.

The structure also contains attributes that inject more information about the contents of a particular element such as a heading or a paragraph.

<h2 lang="en-uk">The Falcon Heavy returned home safely.</h2>

By the name of the attribute, we came to know that it will set the language of the respective heading or a paragraph. Always put the value of an attribute in double quotation marks. I have filled the attribute with UK English. You can add different languages such as French and Spanish in value section.

Imp Note: All attributes cannot be given to all elements in HTML. Some are specific while others are general. The *lang* attribute tends to appear on all elements.

You can find learning HTML handy if you are working at an office as an administrator of a website. You can log into the website as an administrator and edit the code as per your need. You can change the title, put in more attributes, and add more content. I hope you have understood by now that HTML is all about creating text for the web pages.

You might have a question on your mind that whatever is in the HTML code is text but why can't we see everything that is in the editor. You can format the text as per your wishes.

<h1> Elon Musk Dispatched Tesla Stroller to The Space</h1>

<h2> Elon Musk Dispatched Tesla Stroller to The Space</h2>

<h3> Elon Musk Dispatched Tesla Stroller to The Space</h3>

<h4> Elon Musk Dispatched Tesla Stroller to The Space</h4>

<h5> Elon Musk Dispatched Tesla Stroller to The Space</h5>

<h6> Elon Musk Dispatched Tesla Stroller to The Space</h6>

The above are six text sizes for the headings. The h1 being the biggest and h6 being the smallest. That's how it goes on. Please note that you will see all the headings in one size inside the editor but the browser will read them as per the codes. It will display each heading according to the size you assign each of them.

As you have seen in the very first code example that I

have placed the paragraphs for each heading inside the <p></p> tags. No matter how long the paragraph becomes you can put it inside the tags. Let's delve deeper into the text formatting with the help of HTML. If you want a particular word or phrase to look bold in the browser, you can do that with simple tags.

<h1> Elon Musk Dispatched <b>Tesla Stroller</b> to The Space</h1>

The symbol *b* by default means bold. I know what you are thinking right now. Yes, you can make the text italic by inserting the following tags.

<h1> Elon Musk Dispatched <i>Tesla Stroller</i> to The Space</h1>

If you want your text to be displayed by breaking a line, you can do that by inserting the following tags.

<h1> Elon Musk Dispatched Tesla Stroller
 to The Space</h1>

Elon Musk Dispatched Tesla Stroller

to The Space

This is how it will be displayed. Unlike others the break line tag is a single tag. Coupled with this fact is the breaking of sections in the content. Let's do that with the <hr /> tag.

<p> Elon Musk Dispatched Tesla Stroller to The Space</p>

<hr />

<p>The Falcon Heavy has returned to planet Earth</p>

The tag will separate the two with the help of a rule.

Elon Musk Dispatched Tesla Stroller to The Space

The Falcon Heavy has returned to planet Earth

If you want to show a piece of text elevated in importance than others, you can use the <strong> tag.

<p>Elon Musk Dispatched <strong>Tesla Stroller</strong> to The Space</p>

Elon Musk Dispatched **Tesla Stroller** to The Space

Now try this one.

<p>Elon Musk Dispatched <emp>Tesla Stroller</emp> to The Space</p>

Here the tag <emp> means emphasis. You might be thinking that <strong> and <emp> are just the bold and italic tags. Yes, they work like that, but there are slight differences when it comes to getting read by the browser. That's why you should keep in mind these nuances in order to be an efficient coder.

Use <q> and </q> marks to add double quotation marks in a text.

<p>Elon Musk Dispatched <q>Tesla Stroller</q> to The Space</p>

Elon Musk Dispatched "Tesla Stroller" to The Space

List and Images

The sunlight had pierced through the clouds on a muggy morning and now the city had lit up with brilliant sunshine. The clouds, after threshing the city with a record rainfall, were no more overcasting the sky. I got up, had my breakfast, and got ready to go out. Stuck on the door I found a list of eatables that I had to bring home in the evening. Stuffing it in my pocket I left for Abby's home where I was expecting to get my next lesson on HTML. Coincidentally, we had to study lists that day. Abby was pretty excited to teach that. "There are around two major types of lists in HTML," she started.

First of all, there are ordered lists with numbers for each item. They are easy to scan and present. For example, if you want to include a list of exports of a country, you can place them in an ordered list for the users to easily scan it.

Secondly, there are unordered lists which usually come with bullet points.

Learning to form lists is the easiest in HTML. Let's create an ordered list.

```
<ol>
<li>oranges</li>
<li>apples</li>
<li>peach</li>
<li>potatoes</li>
<li>tomatoes</li>
</ol>
```

I took the liberty to fill in the HTML list with all the items that my mom wrote on that list I was talking about. See the result when a browser reads it.

1. oranges
2. apples
3. peach
4. potatoes
5. tomatoes

Let's create an unordered list.

<ul>

<li>oranges</li>

<li>apples</li>

<li>peach</li>

<li>potatoes</li>

<li>tomatoes</li>

</ul>

See the result.

- oranges
- apples
- peach
- potatoes
- tomatoes

If you are a high school teacher, you might know that students frequently demand lists of definitions for learning purposes. Either you can type them and print them on papers to distribute, or you write them on the white board in the classroom or integrate them in a presentation. Or there is a better way. You can upload them on your website. Let's create a list of definitions.

```
<dl>
```

```
<dt>Whale</dt>
```

```
<dd>Whale is the biggest living animal on the planet.
In the past whale oil was used as fuel.</dd>
```

```
<dt>Eagle</dt>
```

```
<dd>Eagle is among the bird species which are known
to be high-flyers. They rest on top of the mountains
and prey on snakes and other littler birds. Such a
class!</dd>
```

```
</dl>
```

Apart from lists, you can also add images to your webpage. As a teacher, Abby had developed a website to which she used to add graphs, charts, and illustrations to explain certain topics to her students. As a website developer, you should create a dedicated folder in your personal computer to store relevant images which you may later on add in the HTML code.

```
<html>
```

```
<img    src-"pictures/penguins.jpg"    alt-"Penguins
singing songs" title-"Penguins usually live in freezing
temperatures."
```

```
</html>
```

The important thing to remember is the name of the image. You should write it accurately in the code so that it would function properly. The word "picture" indicates the name of the folder in which I have stored the relevant image. Please carefully put in the slash then write the name of the image, insert a dot and enter the type of the image. You can guess the type of the image by going into its properties.

The alt section contains a brief description of the image and the title section contains any extra information about the image that you want to add.

You can customize the height and width of the image by the following code.

```
<html>

<img    src-"pictures/penguins.jpg"    alt-"Penguins singing songs" width-"800" height-"500" />

</html>
```

Tricks to draw tables and forms

You can also draw tables in HTML by following some simple steps. For that purpose, we have <table> tags.

```
<html>

<table>

<tr>

<th></th>

<th scope="col">Mission Impossible</th>

<th scope="col">Fast & Furious</th>

<th scope="col">Kungfu Panda</th>

</tr>

<tr>

<th scope="row">Box office collection (US):</th>
```

```
<td>$200m</td>
<td>$150m</td>
<td>$100m</td>
</tr>
<tr>
<th       scope="row">Box       office       collection
(worldwide):</th>
<td>$500m</td>
<td>$400m</td>
<td>$300m</td>
</tr>
</table>
</html>
```

The browser will show it as the following:

	Mission Impossible	Fast & Furious	Kungfu Panda
Box office collection (US):	$200m	$150m	$100m
Box office collection (world):	$500m	$400m	$300m

In the code, *tr* means table row and *td* means table data. The *th* and *td* tags are similar in the sense that both represent the table data but different because *th* is used specifically for headings as it makes the text bold.

Suppose you have some information that has to span over multiple columns and rows. You can use the *span* feature. Abby made use of that feature to set up her tables for displaying on her website. With a simple change in the code, you can make such a table.

```html
<hmtl>
<table>
<tr>
<th></th>
<th>8am</th>
<th>9am</th>
<th>10am</th>
<th>11am</th>
<th>12pm</th>
</tr>
<tr>
<th>Wednesday</th>
<td colspan="2">English Literature</td>
<td>Geology</td>
<td>Economics</td>
<td>Chemistry</td>
</tr>
<tr>
<th>Friday</th>
<td colspan="4">Biology</td>
<td>Taxonomy</td>
</tr>
```

```
</table>
```

```
</hmtl>
```

(Duckett, 2011)

The above table suggests that the browser will display English Literature spanning over two columns titled 8am and 9am. In the second row, the subject Biology will span over four columns, which means Abby will teach the subject for four hours until 12 pm. Let's create another table with length and width properly mentioned.

```
<table width="500" cellpadding="20"
cellspacing="10">
```

```
<tr>
```

```
<th width="200"></th>
```

```
<th>Cars</th>
```

```
<th>Motorbike</th>
```

```
<th width="200">Trailer</th>
```

```
</tr>
```

```
<tr>
```

```
<th>Mercedez Benz</th>
```

```
<td>$1m</td>
```

```
<td>$0.5m</td>
```

```
<td>$3m</td>
```

```
</tr>
```

```
<tr>
```

```
<th>BMW</th>
<td>$1.5m</td>
<td>$1m</td>
<td>$4m</td>
</tr>
</table>
```

By forms the first thing that comes to mind is that you will have to fill it in. You can easily create online forms in HTML for your users or customers to fill in the information you need from them in order to conduct a specific transaction. Forms can be used for entering passwords, email address, searching something online, or simply entering personal information as demanded by the website owner.

Let's create a form that will prompt users to enter their favorite food and favorite drink.

```
<html>
<form action="http://www.cooperfood.com/userfavorites.php">
<p>Favorite Food:
<input type="text" name="favorite food" size="25"
maxlength="40" />
</p>
<p>Favorite Drink:
<input type="text" name="favorite drink" size="25"
```

maxlength="40" />

</p>

</form>

</hmtl>

You have the power to decide the length of the input boxes and the input type. If you replace the input type space with password, the text you as a user will enter will appear in dots just like a password looks like. In addition, you can manage the size and length of the boxes.

An interesting option in creating tables is integrating in your code a radio button. That's fun and smart, and it adds to the glamour of your web page. Let's see the structure for adding a radio button.

<html>

<form action="http://www.foodup.com/home.php">

<p>Please choose your favorite food:

<input type="radio" name="genre" value="sandwich"

checked="checked" /> Sandwich

<input type="radio" name="genre" value="beef steak" />

Beef Steak

<input type="radio" name="genre" value="beef

burger" />

Beef Burger

<input type="radio" name="genre" value="Pizza" />

Pizza

</p>

</form>

</html>

The thing to note is the checked feature of the structure of this code. This suggests that when the page loads, one option will be automatically selected. You can change it once the loading completes. Another important thing is that the checked attribute can only be given to just one feature.

Another interesting type of form is the check box. You might have come across this type of forms while filling out an online application form. Now you can create your own by following a simple structure.

<html>

<form action="http://www.foodup.com/cutomerservice.php">

<p>Please select your delivery mode:

<input type="checkbox" name="service"

value="home delivery" checked="checked" /> Home Delivery

```
<input type="checkbox" name="service"
value="Office delivery" /> Office Delivery
<input type="checkbox" name="service"
value="super urgent to wherever you like" /> Super
Urgent To Wherever You Like
</p>
</form>
</html>
```

You should have understood by now that you can introduce changes to the form structure by changing the input type, the name, and the value. Mostly, the form remains the same for radio buttons and checkboxes. Now I'll try something different with the structure and the result will be a dropdown list, which always looks cool on the website.

```
<html>
<form
action="http://www.foodup.com/home.php">
<p>What food item do like the most at our
restaurant?</p>
<select name="food items">
<option value="super big steak">Super Big
Steak</option>
<option value="sneaky sandwich">Sneaky
Sandwich</option>
<option value="mushrooms">Mushrooms</option>
<option value="chocolate cake">Chocolate
```

Cake</option>

</select>

</form>

</html>

Your customers will find an interactive dropdown list and will be able to choose the desired option to proceed further. Another type of form submission is the submit button by which you can submit your form after you have filled it. Usually, it is a part of most of the application forms. You also use it to subscribe to a website's email network for receiving their newsletters. The structure for the form is as below:

<html>

<form action="http://www.foodup.com/formsubmission.php">

<p>Subscribe yourselves to our company's email list:</p>

<input type="text" name="your email" />

<input type="submit" name="add on" value="Ad" />

</form>

</html>

(Duckett, 2011)

HTML Classes

Let's see how to create classes in HTML.

```html
<!DOCTYPE html>
<html>
<head>
<style>
.cities {
  background-color: black;
  color: white;
  margin: 30px;
  padding: 30px;
}
</style>
</head>
<body>

<div class="countries">
  <h2>The United States of America</h2>
  <p>I am planning to visit The United States of America next year</p>
</div>
```

```
<div class="countries">
 <h2>The Netherlands</h2>
 <p> I am planning to visit The Netherlands next
years</p>
</div>


<div class="countries">
 <h2>Holland</h2>
 <p> I am planning to visit Holland next years </p>
</div>


</body>
</html>
```

It is important to note that you cannot learn just by reading. Practice is very important if you want to be an expert in HTML coding.

Chapter 12:
Exploring the World
of Java

Java is considered as one of the top computer languages that have successfully transformed the world of programming. It was first released in 1995. Since then, it has been radically transforming and even revolutionizing the web. All the dynamics we can find on the web can be attributed to the existence of Java around the web space. The best part about Java was that it evolved quite fast as compared to other computer programming languages. It kept on introducing new features for the users.

Its creators never back down from innovation and that's why we have consistent and some very significant upgrades to Java. Some of them added significantly to the libraries while others attempted to configure the old elements of the library. As the world is getting more integrated, computing is being reshaped across the continents. Java has revolutionized programming. Java is like other languages and is built on the foundations provided by C and C++ languages. What made it stand apart from the other languages is its tendency to keep adding more features and refining itself.

In fact, Java came to replace C++ which made it pretty hard for a programmer to build programs. Programmers needed compilers for building programs with C++, which were not only expensive but also very much time-consuming. The necessity of an easier path cultivated the land for the growth of Java which could produce code that could run on a wide range of differing CPU environments.

Package Declaration

Every file that you compile tends to start with the declaration of the package. The package may consist of multiple numbers and letters. You can also put dots inside them. You need to pack up the package with the application name and also the purpose of the classes you are about to use in the code.

You can add different digits and numbers in the package that indicate the domain of the application you are using, the scope of the code you are creating, the purpose of the classes you will create in the code, and the advanced level of the purpose of classes.

Data Types

Like the other programming languages, Java has a dedicated set of data types. It is a strictly typed language which means compilers check its type compatibility to ensure there are least errors and an improved readability. You will not find any type-less variable in Java.

Primitive data types

The primitive data types of Java help construct the other data types of Java. Let's take a look at them.

Data Type	The Size	The Description
Long	8 bytes	This data type is responsible for storing whole numbers between the ranges: -9, 223, 372, 036, 854, 775, 808 to 9, 223, 372, 036, 854, 775, 807
Byte	1 byte	This data type stores whole numbers ranging from -128 to 127.
Float	4 bytes	This data type stores numbers in fractions. Its storing capacity is 6-7 decimal digits.
Int	4 bytes	This data type stores the whole numbers ranging from -2, 147, 483, 648 to 2, 147, 483, 647.
char	2 bytes	This data type stores just one letter, character or ASCII values.
Double	8 bytes	This data type tends to store the numbers in fractions. Its storing capacity is up to 15 decimal digits.
boolean	1 bit	As in other programming languages boolean tends to store true or false values in Java

Data Type	The Size	The Description
Short	2 bytes	You can store whole numbers in this data type ranging from -32, 768, to 32, 767

(Java Data Types, n.d)

There is a range defined for each type of data. These ranges and values remain the same in every execution environment owing to portability of Java. You won't be needing separate code for different platforms.

```
public class MyClass {
        public static void main(String args[]) {
        int x=50;
        int y=75;
        int z=x*y;
        System.out.println("Sum of x*y = " + z);
        }
}
```

The result we have when we run the Java code in the compiler: Sum of x*y = 3750

I used the inti integer because the data type can store a bigger range of whole numbers as compared to other integers.

Data Operators in Java

You can use operators in order to perform certain operations. There are basically two types of characters in Java: operators and operands. First of all, we will analyze the arithmetic data operators

Addition	This data operator adds the values of a and b	a + b
Subtraction	This arithmetic variable subtracts the value of x from that of y.	x - y
Multiplication	This one multiples a and b.	a * b
Division	This data variable is used to divides the a from b	a / b
Modulus	This data variable returns a remainder	x % y
Increment	This increases the value of x variable by 1	++x
Decrement	It is the opposite of increment as apparent from the name. This cuts the value of a variable by 1	--x

Let's move on to the assignment operators.

Name of the operator	Example	What it means
=	a = 10	a=10
-=	a-=3	a=a-3

/=	a/=3	a=a/3
*=	a*=15	a=a*3
+=	b+=4	b=b+3
%=	a%=3	a=a%3
<<=	x<<=10	x=x<<10
>>=	b>>=15	b=b>>15
|=	a|=5	a=a|5

Have a look at the logical operators.

- !   Logical not   Its job is to reverse the result. For example, if the condition is true, it will return false, and vice versa.
- &&   Logical and   Its job is to return true value if only both statements happen to be true.
- || Logical or   Its job is to return true if just one condition happens to be true. (Java Operators, n.d)

Non-Primitive Data Types

These are also dubbed as reference types because they function by referring back to objects. We have seen that the primitive data types had fixed values that could not be changed. Unlike them, non-primitive data types can be created or changed by the programmer. You can use them to perform certain operations.

The key difference: one notable difference between the two data types is that primitive data type starts with a lowercase while non-primitive data type starts with an uppercase. Let's breakdown the non-primitive types.

Java Strings

A string is used to store text. You can identify a text through the double quotation marks.

```java
public class MyClass {
    public static void main(String[] args) {
        String txt = "Jasmine has enchanting fragrance";
        System.out.println(txt.toLowerCase());
        System.out.println(txt.toUpperCase());
        System.out.println("The length of the txt string is: " + txt.length());
    }
}
```

JASMINE HAS ENCHANTING FRAGRANCE.

jasmine has enchanting fragrance.

The length of the txt string is: 33

Now, we know that we can assign a value to the string. Everything seems fine up till now except that we cannot assign multiple values to a single string. This will take us to another non-primitive data types namely Java Arrays. These arrays are used to store more than one value.

```java
public class MyClass {
```

```java
public static void main(String[] args) {

    String[] flowers = {"Jasmine", "Rose", "Tulip", "Daisy"};

    System.out.println(flowers[0]);

}
}
```

(Java Arrays, n.d)

We have stored four values in a single string. By running this code, you will see the value of the name of the first flower printed out on the screen. If you enter 1 instead of 0 in the line starting with the word system, you will print the second flower name and so on.

You can add the following line to know about the length of the string:

System.out.println(flowers.length);

Types of Objects

Java consists of different classes which serve as templates for the creation of different objects. The process of creation of an object in Java is dubbed as instantiation, and the newly created object is dubbed as an instance of the class which helped in its creation. You can also create objects with templates other than classes. Let's see how they are used to create objects in Java.

Classes

Let's try to create a class based on the model of a car. You can add many attributes the cars as you like. I'll add some to show you how it is done.

package JavaApplication;

public class Car {

      String name;

      int speed:

}

In the above code, I have written different fields for the class. I have used the Java String feature for displaying the name of the model of the car because the name is written in the form of text, for which String is the most appropriate type. Similarly, as the speed will be in a numerical digit, I have used the *int* type for the purpose. The int means an integer. So, it is very simple to understand. You can build any class by this code.

Now that we have successfully created a class, it is time to learn how to use it. For the purpose we need a main () method and also we need to instantiate this class. Let's create a car in the following code.

package JavaApplication;

public class BasicCarDemo {

      public statis void main(String... args) {

      Car car = new Car();

```
car.model = "Audi";

car.speed = 120

}
```

}

I created a *Car* instance for which I made use of the keyword *new*. After that, I have called a special method named as constructor. This method has special status because the compiler automatically generated it. It is pertinent to mention here that you cannot create a class without the constructor.

The Class Variables

In the above code we can add what is missing, which is the average number of years a car survives with an owner.

```
package JavaApplication;

public class Car {

        static final int SURVIVAL = 20;

        String name;

        int speed;

}
```

Almost all the cars have the same average survival rate with an owner. Suppose you are creating objects for around 500 cars. If you have to fill in the survival years of all cars with the same value, it would not be a wise thing to do as it would cost valuable time and labor. That's why you need to be smart and create a special variable named as a constant. So, we have created the new Car class which will run the same rigid value through the code for the entire program. We call this variable a class variable (Cosmina, 2018).

Enumerations and Annotations

Enumerations are represented by the keyword *enum* which is a special class. Enumerations are representatives of a group of constants.

package JavaApplication;

public enum Car {

       BLACK;

       WHITE:

    COLORLESS

}

An enum class is final and cannot be extended. As a special class type, an enum has fields and constructors.

Java If-Else Statements

Like other sophisticated programming languages, Java also supports mathematical conditions.

- a<b denotes that a is less than b.
- a>b denotes that a is greater than b
- a>= b denotes that a is greater or equal to b
- a<=b denotes that it is lesser as well as equal to b
- a != b denotes that it unequal to b
- a == b denotes that it has equal value to that of b.

```java
public class MathOp {
  public static void main(String[] args) {
        if (100 > 40) {

        System.out.println("100 has greater value
than 40"); // obviously

        }
  }
}
```

Another mathematical operation can go like this one:

```java
public class MathOp {
  public static void main(String[] args) {
        int a = 100;
        int b = 40;
        if (a > b) {

        System.out.println("a has greater value than
b");

        }
  }
}
```

Now, let's use Java's ability to perform logical decision and do something interesting.

```java
public class MyClass {
  public static void main(String[] args) {
        int time = 21;
```

```java
        if (time < 17) {
        System.out.println("Have a good day!");
        } else {
        System.out.println("Have a nice evening!");
        }
    }
}
```

You can time your greeting messages for your customers and staff. That's how Java can be automated and power different mobile apps and web apps. Now I'll show you how to use else-if statements.

```java
public class MathOp {
  public static void main(String[] args) {
        int time = 20;
        if (time < 9) {
        System.out.println("Good morning! Have a
nice day!");
        } else if (time < 15) {
        System.out.println("Have a good day!");
        } else {
        System.out.println("Good evening! Have a fun
time with family!");
        }
  }
}
```

The system will show these three results based on if the conditions appear true.

Good morning! Have a nice day!

Have a good day!

Good evening! Have a fun time with family!

I have used 20-hours period in a day to create the above example. If you are exploring the system before 9 hours, it will show you the first statement. If the time exceeds 9 hours but is still less than 15, you will be greeted with the second statement. If it passes 15, you will be greeted with the third statement. This system is fully automated (Java If ... Else, n.d).

Chapter 13:
Something to Talk
About C++

You have to compile C++ in a compiler, which makes it different from the other modern programming languages. You have to first write the code and run it afterwards by a compiler. The compiled files, technically named as object files, are paired up with the help of a linker in order to create a program that could be executed.

A single program may contain one object file or more than one in the form of a combination as per requirement of the program. If there is more than one file, they are usually linked by a linker before execution. C++ programs, unlike most modern programming languages, cannot be exported to other computer systems. They are made specific to a particular computer system. Let's take a look at the core features of C++ programming language.

There are core features of C++ like char and int. In addition, there are loops which consist of for and while statements. The other entities of C++ include standard-library components like vector and map which fall into the category of containers, and I/O which include << and getline(). So, these are the basic features of C++. It is static so the compiler must know the type of every entity you enter in the source file. After it has recognized the type of an object, it gets a sense of what operations it has to apply on it.

Starting from the basics

Let's create the first C++ file.

#include <iostream>

using namespace std;

int main() {

        cout<< "Angels are falling from the heavens.";

        return 0;

}

We have successfully defined a function called main. You can see the {} brackets which indicate the start and end of a function. This function is an inseparable part of all the programs that we will execute in C++. If you run the above-written command on a C++ compiler, apart from what you have put in the double quotation marks, you will see the following text on the console screen.

Program finished with exit code 0

Press ENTER to exit console.

This suggests that the function must return the zero value for successful execution of the program. You can say that the function executes everything it was expected to and likewise returns the zero value to the console. If the value is not zero, the execution definitely fails. So, for successful execution each time, the returned value must be zero.

Another thing you can see in the function is #include <iostream>. This is actually an instruction for the compiler so that it could include the declarations of Input and Output facilities that are found in the iostream. The second line of the function using namespace std suggests that the programmer has the freedom to utilize objects as well as variables which are available in the standard lib. Both these lines are going to get into all of your programs so you should get used to them. Next comes an empty line. It doesn't matter how many empty lines you have to enter the code; C++ just ignores these whitespaces. So, don't worry about them. In languages such as Python, you cannot ignore a whitespace, but C++ cares little about them. One less thing to worry about for programmers.

The word count denoted the I/O (input and output) text in the code. You might have noticed a ; in the function. Every statement ends with it. One important thing to keep in mind is that you can write the entire main function in a single line once you get used to the compiler. This is something that I cannot recommend to beginners because it will be much more difficult to read and understand your own code, let alone edit it.

Let's define some of the words that you would come across while learning the C language.

- A value is in the form of bits that are interpreted according to a particular type.
- A type carries information on possible values and operations for an object.

- An object carries value of some type.
- If we name an object, it is called a variable.

In addition, there are different types of fundamentals given, as below:

- int   //this refers to integers such as 1,2,3, 456 or 9999.
- bool   // as evident from the short form, this one refers to Boolean. It has just two possible values: true and false.
- double   //this refers to the floating-point numbers such as 5.999 and 3.567.

I have already said that C++ is not portable to other systems when you have created a program on a particular system. Now, I am telling you the reason for that. All the fundamental types I have discussed above remain in direct correspondence with the hardware of the computer system, so naturally, they have to adapt to the system to execute a particular program. All these variables have set capacity for storing information. For example, one char is capable of storing a single character of 8-byte size on a particular computer system.

C++ has different arithmetical operators given as below:

```
+x            //This is unary plus

x+y           // This is simple plus

x/y           // This indicates division

−x            // This indicates unary minus

x*y           // This suggests multiplication in a program
```

179

x−y   // This is simple minus

x%y   // This is remainder for integers (modulus)

You might be wondering what these backslashes are for. As you might have already guessed, they are used in the code to write comments for your own memory and understanding. Now I have to move on to the comparison operators (Strousturp, n.d).

x<=y   // This denotes less than or equal in a comparison

x==y   // This is the equal sign

x>=y   // This denotes greater than or equal comparison

x<y   // This is for less than

x>y   // This is used to denote greater than

x!=y   // This is used to denote not equal

An important thing to conclude this section is that you can do away with the using namespace std line in the code. It can be replaced with the following. Let's see the code that we had created earlier on and replace the line with a single keyword std.

#include <iostream>

int main() {

   std::cout << "Angels are falling from the heavens.";

   return 0;

}

(C++ Getting Started, n.d)

The output of this code will be the same.

Computation

We can create our own variables. Let's try one.

```
#include <iostream>
using namespace std;
int main() {
  int myFif;
  myFif = 25;
  cout << myFif;
  return 0;
}
```

I have created a new variable myFif and assigned it a value 25. If later on I decide to assign myFif a new value or by mistake I reassign myFif a new value, it will override the first instead of turning out error.

```
#include <iostream>
using namespace std;
int main() {
  int myFif = 25;   // I assign myFif the number 25
  myFif = 50;       // I assign myFif the number 50
  cout << myFif;
```

```
  return 0;

}
```

You will see that the variable myFif carries 50 as a value. You can stop this overriding tendency of the compiler by making your variable a constant.

```
#include <iostream>

using namespace std;

int main() {

  const int myFif = 25;

  myFif = 50;

  cout << myFif;

  return 0;

}
```

You will get the following message in the console:

main.cpp: In function 'int main()':

main.cpp:6:11: error: assignment of read-only variable 'myFif'

```
    myFif = 50;
```

Strings, Statements, and Loops

You can create strings in C++ language in order to store data in the form of text. If you are learning other programming languages, this might seem familiar to you.

```
#include <iostream>
```

```cpp
#include <string>

using namespace std;

int main() {

  string greeting = "Angels are falling from the heavens.";

  cout << greeting;

  return 0;
}
```

If you are creating a program for a user who will enter their car names and model numbers in the boxes and you store the information. The information you need cannot be received in a single box, as it will not only confuse the user, but also yourself as you won't be able to distinguish between the two. That will make storing the data quite a tough job. So, the solution is to create separate boxes for the two values. When you receive two separate pieces of information, you can pair them up with the help of the process of concatenation.

Let's try one. You can run the following string concatenation function on the compiler you have installed on your computer system.

```cpp
#include <iostream>

#include <string>

using namespace std;

int main () {
```

```
string carName = "Audi ";

string carModel = "Flame";

string carInfo = carName + carModel;

cout << carInfo;

return 0;
}
```

You will see the result: *Audi Flame*. This program can help you streamline a lot of customer service projects in which we seek their information and store it in our databases. Also, you can pair up more than one strings to store information. We can change individual characters in a string.

```
#include <iostream>

#include <string>

using namespace std;

int main() {

string myFif = "Angels are falling from the heavens.";

myFif[0] = 'A';

myFif[1] = 'P';

myFif[2] = 'P';

myFif[3] = 'L';

myFif[4] = 'E';

myFif[5] = 'S';

cout << myFif;
```

```
  return 0;

}
```

Apples are falling from the heavens.

The above should be the result that you are watching on the console screen. That's how you can edit and modify the text of a string in case a user has entered wrong spellings or has missed an alphabet altogether.

```
#include <iostream>

#include <string>

using namespace std;

int main() {

  string carName;

  cout << "Enter the name of your favorite car: ";

  getline (cin, carName);

  cout << "Your favorite car name is: " << carName;

  return 0;

}
```

Enter the name of your favorite car: BMW

Your favorite car name is: BMW

This will be the result. You will be asked to enter your favorite car name. In my case, it is the famous BMW, so I entered the same and received the instant output. This is a simple program to create a user input box in your C++ program. Things have started getting exciting by now, haven't they? This is a practical application of C++ (C++ Strings, n.d).

Statements

Like other programming languages, you can direct your program to make a certain decision on the basis of the input you give to the compiler. I'm moving towards taking the if statement and pushing it into the compiler to see how it works. Let's create an if statement.

```
#include <iostream>

using namespace std;

int main() {
  int x = 555;
  int y = 355;
  int z = 200;
  if (x+y > z) {
        cout << "x has greater value than that of z";
  }
  return 0;
}
```

The output is definitely: x has greater value than that of z. Let's see if it turns out to be wrong.

```
#include <iostream>

using namespace std;
```

```cpp
int main() {
  int x = 5;
  int y = 10;
  int z = 200;
  if (x+y > z) {
        cout << "x has greater value than that of z";
  }
  return 0;
}
```

The output will be a blank page on the console. The condition remained false that's why the compiler didn't return any response. The reason behind a blank screen is that we have left a void in the if statement. We didn't tell her what to do if the condition turned out to be false. This brings us to the if-else statement.

```cpp
#include <iostream>
using namespace std;
int main() {
  int time = 1;
  if (time < 12) {
        cout << "Have a delightful day!";
  } else {
        cout << "Enjoy the lovely evening!";
  }
```

```
    return 0;

}
```

(C++ If ... Else, n.d)

Now let's move on to the else-if statement in which you can put multiple conditions.

```
#include <iostream>

using namespace std;

int main() {

  int date = 31;

  if (date < 25) {

        cout << "You are well in time. You can submit
your application form.";

  } else if (date < 29 ) {

        cout << "You are late. Make if fast or you will
miss the deadline.";

  } else {

        cout << "You cannot submit the application.";

  }

  return 0;

}
```

They will be the last sentence if the user gets late and submits the application after 31st. Please don't forget to update the date of your computer system before writing, compiling, and executing this conditional statement.

```cpp
#include <iostream>
using namespace std;

int main() {
  for (int z = 5; z < 20; z++) {
        cout << z << "\n";
  }
  return 0;
}
```

In the above code, I gave the compiler directions to run on its own after forming a loop that would run through the whole code until it satisfies the condition that I had put in. You will grasp it easily once you see how the loop runs through the entire code. The following list will appear on the screen of the console.

5

6

7

8

9

10

11

12

13

14

15

16

17

18

19

The exhausted itself until the conditions in the statement are fulfilled.

Functions

You have to create a function and call it to run it in the compiler. You can use functions to do a specific job for you. What do you need to do to use the function in C++? First of all, declare the function. You can assign it a certain type of value. A function may carry multiple statements which are executed in an orderly manner. If you remember from the start, I talked about the *main* function, about which I told you that it would be a part of all C++ programs. If you want to see how a function looks, you can refer back to it.

When the compiler gets a function call, it temporarily puts a halt on the current function and runs the one that is called.

#include <iostream>

using namespace std;

void myFunct1() {

   cout << "This user is not on the line at the moment.

Please try later.";

}

int main() {

 myFunct1();

  return 0;

}

This user is not on the line at the moment. Please try later.

You can see that I have declared the function titled as myFunct1 in the compiler. Then I have called it through the main function. You can call a function anytime as per will or need. This function can be used in a program where a customer tries to contact a user who is offline. The function is immediately called as per its coding and conditions. You can use a true and false statement here in order to call the function if the condition turns out to be true.

Let's suppose that the customer keeps on calling. In that case, the function can be repeatedly called just like the following. Each time it is called, it conveys the same message.

#include <iostream>

using namespace std;

void myFunct1() {

  cout << "This user is not on the line at the moment. Please try later.";

}

```cpp
int main() {
  myFunct1();
  myFunct1();
  myFunct1();
  myFunct1();
  myFunct1();
  myFunct1();
  return 0;
}
```

This user is not on the line at the moment. Please try later.

This user is not on the line at the moment. Please try later.

This user is not on the line at the moment. Please try later.

This user is not on the line at the moment. Please try later.

This user is not on the line at the moment. Please try later.

This user is not on the line at the moment. Please try later.

In the above-mentioned example, the customer called the user six times and received the same message. So, that's how C++ can helps us automate simply some very basic tasks.

Chapter 14:
Get the Knowhow
About SQL

The first thing that comes to our minds when we think of Structured Query Language (SQL) is a database. A database is all about information in the form of sets. There are lots of databases around us in our real lives such as a rate list or a telephone directory. Abby keeps one in her home as a piece of memory from the glorious past. When I started learning SQL, she took it out, opened it and handed it over to me. "This is what SQL is all about," she said. The directory had several lists of names, phone numbers, and addresses of inhabitants of a particular state. They were alphabetically ordered.

"Can you find me the telephone number of Mr. John from Harley Street within five seconds," asked Abby. "I can try my best," was my response. Two full minutes had passed and only after that I succeeded in tracking the telephone number of the right person. It was embarrassing to say the least. But as with other embarrassment that too passed anyway. What does that even have to offer? It offered some lessons. The first one was that finding out a telephone number from a manual dictionary was a time-consuming task. Secondly, I had to match the address and the names in order to find the telephone number of the right person. Thirdly, a telephone directory cannot be updated easily that's why it becomes less useful with the passage of time. Not only the telephone directory but almost all manual databases on the planet have similar problems. Updating them is too hard a task to finish fast. It takes loads of cash to be spent on the labor that would update the database (Beaulieu, 2009).

What is SQL?

SQL is a programming language to build a dynamic database. It is divided into different parts that can be individually explored. I will go for the statement classes in the start. By using these statements, you can edit and update your database. For example, you can use the SQL schema statement to create a table in SQL in which you can store information such as a table that would show the models of cars, their prices, and speed range. Let's create a table named corporation by using SQL schema statement.

CREATE TABLE corporation

(corp_id SMALLINT,

name VARCHAR(30)

CONSTRAINT pk_corporation PRIMARY KEY (corp_id)

);

There will be do columns in this table namely corp_id and name. We have identified the corp_id column as the table's primary key (Beaulieu, 2009).

SQL has special tables named as data dictionaries in which the tables that are created with the help of schema statements are stored. You can view these tables by using a select statement. Let's take an example of a banker who is ordered by her boss to store data about newly opened bank accounts in the month of January. The banker stores the information by creating a table using schema statement. Now the month has ended and the table has reached its logical end. Her boss demands from her a full-fledged report at the end of the month of January. One option for her is to use the SELECT statement and retrieve information about each account while the option is to determine the set of columns that the table has and generate a report accordingly.

What is MySQL?

MySQL is a database server on which you can create your own SQL database. A good thing about it is you can download and install it for free. Let's create a table using MySQL. There are certain steps involved in the creation of the table. The very first step is the design of the table. This brings us to the list of supercars that I had talked about earlier on. As a MySQL database operator, you need to think about the contents of the table and then design it accordingly. Our table about the supercars may consist of the following:

- Name of the cars
- Model name of the cars
- Color of the cars

Let's name the columns:

Column	Type
Name of the cars	Varchar(20)
Model Name of the cars	Varchar(30)
Color of the cars	Varchar(30)

Let's create it.

CREATE TABLE supercars (

Name of the cars VARCHAR(20)

Model name of the cars VARCHAR(30)

Color of the cars VARCHAR(30));

It is pertinent to mention here that MySQL commands are usually long as well as complicated therefore should be written on a single line as you will have to add multiple lines, which elevates the chances of your getting confused. The longer the code gets difficult it will be for you to understand and work it out. In order to check whether a new table has been created or not, you need to type the following on the MySQL server.

DESCRIBE supercars;

It will pop up right away. This command can be used to locate errors in the database. You can easily display and find out what is wrong with the data and rectify it.

A brief introduction to SQL

Structured Query Language (SQL) is well-known to do the following tasks.

- It has the ability to update the records that already exist in the database.
- It can draw new tables inside the database to streamline information.
- You can delete the existing records, and insert new ones in the database.
- You can create entirely fresh databases.
- If you run a big business, you can set permissions on tables and certain procedures (Introduction to SQL, n.d).

Relational Database Management System is considered as the base of SQL. A peculiar thing about the RDBMS is that it stores the data in the form of tables. Lots of tables! These tables are basically called database objects. These tables are the same that we have just tried to create in the previous section of this chapter. Tables in SQL contain related data entries. Like normal tables, they too have columns as well as rows. Let's view an example of a table.

SQL> CREATE TABLE ACCOUNTS (

SrNo INT NOT NULL,

AccountNumber int NOT NULL,

Name VARCHAR (25) NOT NULL,

Gender VARCHAR(25) NOT NULL,

Country VARCHAR (30),

);

A usual table may contain information about your customer's identification, his or her name, their credit card details, their phone numbers, their gender, their country or state and any other details which you want to include in the table. You can break down your table into tiny parts which are named as fields.

Sr no.	AccountNumber	Name	Gender	Country
1	8596457	John	Male	Germany
2	126545	Emily	Female	United States
3	748525	Mary	Female	The United Kingdom
4	984578	Edwin	Male	The Netherlands
5	895623	Ashwin	Male	Australia
6	564578	Eric	Male	The United States
7	964578	Jimmy	Male	Switzerland

This table has five fields. Each field has to store a specific information. You might be thinking that I am giving columns a new name. These are called columns, you are right, in a traditional table. The rows in the table of SQL are called records. While columns have information about all the records in their purview, a record is just a single entry in the columns. A record is dubbed as a horizontal entry in the table. Your database may contain a single entry or it may have a thousand tables. It depends on your usage and the size of information you receive every day. Each table name should have a unique name.

In the upcoming table, I'll discuss some arithmetic operators which you can use in SQL to do some simple calculations. I assume that the variables x and y have values 30 and 20, respectively.

Operator	Description	Example
+	This operator is for addition of two variables. It is as simple as doing it on a calculator.	x+y will show 50
-	It is used to subtract one operand from the other operand.	x-y will show 10
*	This operator multiplies the operands.	x*y will show 600
/	This one is used divide one variable by the other operand.	x/y will give 1.5
%	This one is used to divide one from the other and also leave behind a remainder.	x%y will give 6

I have compiled a list of comparison operators in SQL. Please have a read and see what they mean and how you can use these symbols.

Operator	Description	Example
=	This operator checks if the two variables hold equal value or not. If they are equal, only then the condition becomes true.	(x=y) is not true

Operator	Description	Example
!=	This symbol checks the inequality of values between the two operands. It returns the true value only after it confirms inequality of value. In case of equal value, it returns false.	(x!=y) is true
<>	This symbol checks the inequality of values between the two operands. It returns the true value only after it confirms inequality of value. In case of equal value, it returns false.	(x<>y) is true
>	This symbol checks if on variable has greater value than the other. If the left operand has greater value then condition is returned true.	(x>y) is not true
<	This symbol checks if on variable has greater value than the other. The only difference is that it centers around the right side variable. You can read it otherwise. If the value of the left side variable is lesser than that of the right side variable, only then the condition returns true.	(x<y) is true

Operator	Description	Example
>=	This one does two things. It checks if the value of the left-hand variable is greater than or is equal to that of the right-side variable. If yes, then the condition is returned as true.	(x>=y) is not true
<=	This one also does two things. It checks if the value of the right-hand variable is greater than or is equal to that of the left-side variable. If yes, then the condition is returned as true.	(x<=y) is true
!<	This operator checks if the value of the left variable is not less than the right one or not. If it is, then the condition stands true.	(x!<y) is not true
!>	This one works otherwise. It checks if the value of the left variable is not greater than the right one or not. If it is, then the condition stands true.	(x!>y) is true

Let's take a look at some logical operators of SQL.

Operator	Description
ALL	This operator has a job to compare a value to all values in another value set.
AND	This operator makes an SQL statement flexible by allowing the presence of more than one conditions inside one statement.
BETWEEN	You can hunt out values by this operator, that are lying inside a set of values.
NOT	You can use this to reverse the meaning of a logical operator.
OR	This one is special in a sense that it allows you to pair up multiple conditions in your statements.
EXISTS	If you are not sure whether a table contains a record or not, use this operator to confirm.
LIKE	This one uses a wildcard operator and helps compare a particular value with similar values in the database.

(SQL Operator, n.d)

An important thing to know about tables in SQL is that if you create a wrong table or if any of them has a mistake or if a table is old enough to be deleted from the database because you don't need it anymore, you have the option of dropping that table.

Note: Remember it is not recommended to delete even old tables from the database because you can feel the need to see them or use them any time. However, if you have shut down a particular branch of your business, you can delete additional data to ease off load on your database and to make it easier to sift through a few tables that remain.

Let's see how to delete an unwanted table from the database.

DROP TABLE "Accounts";

This statement will delete the entire table from the database. Before you drop the table, it is recommended that you view if it already exists. You should also make sure whether you are deleting the right table from the database. So, use the following command first.

DESC ACCOUNTS;

Sr no.	AccountNumber	Name	Gender	Country
1	8596457	John	Male	Germany
2	126545	Emily	Female	The United States
3	748525	Mary	Female	The United Kingdom
4	984578	Edwin	Male	The Netherlands

Sr no.	AccountNumber	Name	Gender	Country
5	895623	Ashwin	Male	Australia
6	564578	Eric	Male	The United States
7	964578	Jimmy	Male	Switzerland

Now we know that the Accounts table exists in the database, so we can drop it right away. When you have deleted a table, you can check whether it has actually been deleted or not by the DESC command. This was about deleting the entire table from the database. In addition to dropping entire tables, you also can delete individual rows from the table.

DELETE FROM ACCOUNTS

WHERE SrNo = 2;

This will delete the full row that falls under SrNo 2. If you fail to specify the serial number of the rows, the delete command will delete all the rows from your table. So, be careful when you are about to enter the command. See the syntax. It is recommended to use the DESC command at first to confirm which row you need to do away with. Only then should you use the Delete command, so that you don't mistake an important row for the one you want to get rid of. So, SQL is fun to operate. Its ease of use has really revolutionized businesses across the world.

You can delete a single record from the table. Here is the table right now.

Sr no.	Account Number	Name	Gender	Country
1	8596457	John	Male	Germany
2	126545	Emily	Female	The United States
3	748525	Mary	Female	The United Kingdom
4	984578	Edwin	Male	The Netherlands
5	895623	Ashwin	Male	Australia
6	564578	Eric	Male	The United States
7	964578	Jimmy	Male	Switzerland

Let's see the syntax of the delete command.

DELETE FROM Accounts

WHERE Name = 'Mary';

Sr no.	AccountNumber	Name	Gender	Country
1	8596457	John	Male	Germany
2	126545	Emily	Female	United States

Sr no.	AccountNumber	Name	Gender	Country
4	984578	Edwin	Male	The Netherlands
5	895623	Ashwin	Male	Australia
6	564578	Eric	Male	The United States
7	964578	Jimmy	Male	Switzerland

You also can delete multiple records by a single command. Let's see how to do it. We will look at the table how it looked before deletion.

Sr no.	AccountNumber	Name	Gender	Country
1	8596457	John	Male	Germany
2	126545	Emily	Female	The United States
3	748525	Mary	Female	The United Kingdom
4	984578	Edwin	Male	The Netherlands
5	895623	Ashwin	Male	Australia
6	564578	Eric	Male	The United States
7	964578	Jimmy	Male	Switzerland

Now, I'll go on deleting the records.

DELETE FROM Accounts WHERE Country = 'The United States';

Sr no.	AccountNumber	Name	Gender	Country
1	8596457	John	Male	Germany
3	748525	Mary	Female	The United Kingdom
4	984578	Edwin	Male	The Netherlands
5	895623	Ashwin	Male	Australia
7	964578	Jimmy	Male	Switzerland

If you, by mistake, forget to enter the WHERE clause and run the command like the one below, you will wash your hands of the entire table. Let's see how your table looks like before the command. Use DESC command to display the table on your screen.

Sr no.	AccountNumber	Name	Gender	Country
1	8596457	John	Male	Germany
2	126545	Emily	Female	The United States

Sr no.	AccountNumber	Name	Gender	Country
3	748525	Mary	Female	The United Kingdom
4	984578	Edwin	Male	The Netherlands
5	895623	Ashwin	Male	Australia
6	564578	Eric	Male	The United States
7	964578	Jimmy	Male	Switzerland

Now let's run the command.

DELETE FROM Accounts;

Sr no.	AccountNumber	Name	Gender	Country

They will lose their value by a single stroke of the key. It is recommended that you use a dummy SQL table for learning this command. Otherwise, you will lose important data (SQL DELETE Statement, n.d).

Another interesting statement in SQL is the TOP command. It is read in combo with the SELECT clause. Let's see what it can do to our tables. First, I'll show how our table looks like before executing the command.

Sr no.	AccountNumber	Name	Gender	Country
1	8596457	John	Male	Germany
2	126545	Emily	Female	The United States
3	748525	Mary	Female	The United Kingdom
4	984578	Edwin	Male	The Netherlands
5	895623	Ashwin	Male	Australia
6	564578	Eric	Male	The United States
7	964578	Jimmy	Male	Switzerland

Now, I'll write the syntax for the TOP command and see how it can help me.

SELECT TOP 5 * FROM Accounts;

Sr no.	AccountNumber	Name	Gender	Country
1	8596457	John	Male	Germany
2	126545	Emily	Female	The United States
3	748525	Mary	Female	The United Kingdom
4	984578	Edwin	Male	The Netherlands

Sr no.	AccountNumber	Name	Gender	Country
5	895623	Ashwin	Male	Australia

The command has sliced off the last two records of the table. There are limitations when it comes to the TOP command. MySQL doesn't support. It has its own statement for the same job.

MySQL gives us the LIMIT to do the same tasks which the TOP command does.

SELECT * FROM Accounts

LIMIT 5;

Sr no.	AccountNumber	Name	Gender	Country
1	8596457	John	Male	Germany
2	126545	Emily	Female	The United States
3	748525	Mary	Female	The United Kingdom
4	984578	Edwin	Male	The Netherlands
5	895623	Ashwin	Male	Australia

Now let's do that with the ROWNUM statement.

SELECT * FROM Accounts

WHERE ROWNUM 5;

Sr no.	AccountNumber	Name	Gender	Country
1	8596457	John	Male	Germany
2	126545	Emily	Female	The United States
3	748525	Mary	Female	The United Kingdom
4	984578	Edwin	Male	The Netherlands
5	895623	Ashwin	Male	Australia

SQL is more interesting than you think. If you want the top half of the information available, SQL can display that as well. This is how the table looks now.

Sr no.	AccountNumber	Name	Gender	Country
1	8596457	John	Male	Germany
2	126545	Emily	Female	The United States
3	748525	Mary	Female	The United Kingdom
4	984578	Edwin	Male	The Netherlands
5	895623	Ashwin	Male	Australia
6	564578	Eric	Male	The United States

Sr no.	AccountNumber	Name	Gender	Country
7	964578	Jimmy	Male	Switzerland
8	234578	Catly	Female	Romania

See the syntax below.

SELECT TOP 50 PERCENT * FROM Accounts;

Sr no.	AccountNumber	Name	Gender	Country
1	8596457	John	Male	Germany
2	126545	Emily	Female	The United States
3	748525	Mary	Female	The United Kingdom
4	984578	Edwin	Male	The Netherlands

SQL Select Statement

SQL revolves around statements. You can do most of the tasks if you memorize the job of each statement. This is how things start getting smoother. The very first statement that we need to discuss is the SELECT statement. Let's see the syntax for the select statement.

SELECT * FROM Accounts;

I have written the name of a dummy database titled as Accounts. We'll go from here. The select statement actually selects all the existing records in the Accounts table. The following are some key points that you need to keep in mind in order to avoid any errors while drafting and using SQL statements.

First things first. SQL statements are not affected in any way by uppercase or lowercase. It interprets the keyword in the same way whether you write SELECT or select.

Some database systems demand that you put a semicolon at the end of each statement. This requirement is relaxed in some databases. Semicolons actually do more good than harm as they allow programmers to enter multiple statements only separated by a semicolon. This saves time and makes usage of SQL easier.

The SELECT statement is quite interesting as it has made handling tables very easy. You can select a particular data and get it returned in the form of a result-set.

You can select a particular column out of the full table.

Sr no.	AccountNumber	Name	Gender	Country
1	8596457	John	Male	Germany
2	126545	Emily	Female	United States
3	748525	Mary	Female	The United Kingdom
4	984578	Edwin	Male	The Netherlands
5	895623	Ashwin	Male	Australia

Sr no.	AccountNumber	Name	Gender	Country
6	564578	Eric	Male	The United States
7	964578	Jimmy	Male	Switzerland

This table is named as Accounts. If we want to see the list of Account numbers and the Names of account holders, we can use the following statement (SQL SELECT Statement, n.d).

SELECT AccountNumber, Names FROM Accounts;

In general, there are many duplicate values in a table. For example, a single person can have three different accounts in the table. You can go for the option of selecting only distinct values from a particular column in the table.

SELECT DISTINCT AccountNumber, Names FROM Accounts;

To continue with the SELECT statement, I'll move on to the WHERE clause. It is used for specifying a condition when you are selecting a row or a column or even the entire table. If the SQL finds the condition to be fulfilled, it comes back with the specific value that you were looking after for. You can extract only the information you need. This saves you considerable time that you would have consumed on sifting through loads of data only to find the information that you need. The syntax for the WHERE clause is as below:

SELECT AccountNumber, Names

FROM Accounts

WHERE write the condition here;

Here is our table that is stored in the database:

Sr no.	AccountNumber	Name	Gender	Country
1	8596457	John	Male	Germany
2	126545	Emily	Female	The United States
3	748525	Mary	Female	The United Kingdom
4	984578	Edwin	Male	The Netherlands
5	895623	Ashwin	Male	Australia
6	564578	Eric	Male	The United States
7	964578	Jimmy	Male	Switzerland

SELECT * FROM Accounts

WHERE Country='The United States';

The result will be as below:

Sr no.	AccountNumber	Name	Gender	Country
2	126545	Emily	Female	The United States
6	564578	Eric	Male	The United States

The where class has helped me fish out the details I needed from the table without bothering me over finding it manually and jotting it down on paper. This comes handy in large organizations where there are thousands of customer IDs or banks that deal with thousands of bank accounts simultaneously. In addition to maintaining the database, customers keep dropping in all day to get information about their bank accounts. On top of that are the demands of your boss who is always asking for preparing this or that report. If you are unaware of the WHERE clause, you are bound to take a snub from your boss for not preparing the reports well in time. It is just not practical to manually go through all the details and carve out a report. The marvel of SQL has enabled corporations to run in a fast yet highly efficient manner. This is how you can get past your competitors in a highly dynamic business environment.

We have retrieved information through text. Now it is time to retrieve a specific part of that information from the table through numeric values.

SELECT * FROM Accounts

WHERE SrNO=2;

Sr no.	AccountNumber	Name	Gender	Country
2	126545	Emily	Female	The United States

If you have noted the syntax carefully, you might have realized a slight difference between how I retrieved information with the help of text and how I did so with the help of numeric values. SQL demands that you enclose the text value in single quotation marks while leave the numeric values open. Don't use double quotation marks instead of single quotes as SQL will return a syntax error (WHERE Clause Example, n.d).

AND, OR, and NOT in SQL

You can also pair up the WHERE clause with different operators like AND, NOT, and OR. With the help of these operators, you will be able to filter the records by adding multiple conditions. This will help you get far more targeted results. Let's see how these operators work.

The AND operator: You can add multiple conditions separated by AND. It returns the result after checking whether all the conditions that you have put in the WHERE clause are true. If yes, it displays the result.

The OR operator: It displays the result if any one of the conditions of the WHERE clause is true. You have to insert the OR operator just like you put in the AND operators.

On the other hand, the NOT operator only displays the result if your condition remains unfulfilled. See the status of your table as below after that run the OR statement.

Sr no.	AccountNumber	Name	Gender	Country
1	8596457	John	Male	Germany
2	126545	Emily	Female	The United States
3	748525	Mary	Female	The United Kingdom
4	984578	Edwin	Male	The Netherlands
5	895623	Ashwin	Male	Australia
6	564578	Eric	Male	The United States
7	964578	Jimmy	Male	Switzerland

Now, run the following statement.

SELECT * FROM Accounts

WHERE Country='The United States' AND Name='Emily';

Run on the SQL server and see the result.

Sr no.	AccountNumber	Name	Gender	Country
2	126545	Emily	Female	The United States

Now I'll go for the OR operator. I'll use the same dummy table titled as Accounts and try to retrieve information with the help of names while the country remains the same. The table looks like the one.

Sr no.	AccountNumber	Name	Gender	Country
1	8596457	John	Male	Germany
2	126545	Emily	Female	The United States
3	748525	Mary	Female	The United Kingdom
4	984578	Edwin	Male	The Netherlands
5	895623	Ashwin	Male	Australia
6	564578	Eric	Male	The United States
7	964578	Jimmy	Male	Switzerland

See the syntax as below.

SELECT * FROM Accounts

WHERE Name='Emily' OR Name='Eric';

Let's see the result.

Sr no.	AccountNumber	Name	Gender	Country
2	126545	Emily	Female	The United States
6	564578	Eric	Male	The United States

Moving on with the OR operator, let's try some other names.

SELECT * FROM Accounts

WHERE Name='John' OR Name='Eric' OR Name='Edwin' OR Name='Ashwin';

Sr no.	AccountNumber	Name	Gender	Country
1	8596457	John	Male	Germany
4	984578	Edwin	Male	The Netherlands
5	895623	Ashwin	Male	Australia
6	564578	Eric	Male	The United States

Sometimes, we need lots of information except a particular piece which we need to ignore. Suppose you have one hundred rows in a table. You want to exclude five rows and need the other ninety-five. Would you like to create an AND command for the purpose and spend the whole day in drafting it, only to realize in the end that you have committed a syntax error? In a command that long, any unintentional error may happen more often. It is not wise, if not totally absurd. That's why we have the NOT operator, which offers a perfect solution for this problem. Let's use that. Suppose from our Accounts table we don't need information about the account holders of Australia. The table appears as below.

Sr no.	AccountNumber	Name	Gender	Country
1	8596457	John	Male	Germany
2	126545	Emily	Female	The United States
3	748525	Mary	Female	The United Kingdom
4	984578	Edwin	Male	The Netherlands
5	895623	Ashwin	Male	Australia
6	564578	Eric	Male	The United States
7	964578	Jimmy	Male	Switzerland

See the syntax below.

SELECT * FROM Accounts

WHERE NOT Country='Australia';

We will have the following result. SQL will carve out the records that have account holder details from Australia. The rest of the records will be set up in the form of a result set to be displayed on your screen. In this example, we have one record which contains details of account holders from Australia. The same will be omitted by the NOT operator.

Sr no.	AccountNumber	Name	Gender	Country
1	8596457	John	Male	Germany

Sr no.	AccountNumber	Name	Gender	Country
2	126545	Emily	Female	The United States
3	748525	Mary	Female	The United Kingdom
4	984578	Edwin	Male	The Netherlands
6	564578	Eric	Male	The United States
7	964578	Jimmy	Male	Switzerland

You can use these three operators in conjunction with one another. Let's combine them in a command. Keep in mind the real form of the table as below, then we will move on to see the changes.

Sr no.	AccountNumber	Name	Gender	Country
1	8596457	John	Male	Germany
2	126545	Emily	Female	The United States
3	748525	Mary	Female	The United Kingdom
4	984578	Edwin	Male	The Netherlands
5	895623	Ashwin	Male	Australia
6	564578	Eric	Male	The United States
7	964578	Jimmy	Male	Switzerland

Let's see how it works.

SELECT * FROM Accounts

WHERE NOT Country='Australia' AND NOT Country='Switzerland';

Let's see the result of the command.

Sr no.	AccountNumber	Name	Gender	Country
1	8596457	John	Male	Germany
2	126545	Emily	Female	The United States
3	748525	Mary	Female	The United Kingdom
4	984578	Edwin	Male	The Netherlands
6	564578	Eric	Male	The United States

Your desired result set is short of the two rows which you have put in the NOT command. Let's move on to combine the other two operators in the next syntax.

SELECT * FROM Accounts

WHERE Country='The United States' AND (Name='Emily' OR City='Eric');

Run it on the SQL server and see the result as below:

Sr no.	AccountNumber	Name	Gender	Country
2	126545	Emily	Female	The United States
6	564578	Eric	Male	The United States

(SQL AND, OR and NOT Operators, n.d)

SQL Order By

This keyword is used to sort out the result of a table in its ascending as well as descending order. For directing SQL to move in the ascending or descending order, you can use ASC or DESC keywords. The original form of the table is as below.

Sr no.	AccountNumber	Name	Gender	Country
1	8596457	John	Male	Germany
2	126545	Emily	Female	The United States
3	748525	Mary	Female	The United Kingdom
4	984578	Edwin	Male	The Netherlands
5	895623	Ashwin	Male	Australia
6	564578	Eric	Male	The United States
7	964578	Jimmy	Male	Switzerland

Let's see the syntax and run it on SQL.

SELECT * FROM Accounts

ORDER BY Country;

Sr no.	AccountNumber	Name	Gender	Country
5	895623	Ashwin	Male	Australia
1	8596457	John	Male	Germany
7	964578	Jimmy	Male	Switzerland
4	984578	Edwin	Male	The Netherlands
3	748525	Mary	Female	The United Kingdom
6	564578	Eric	Male	The United States
2	126545	Emily	Female	The United States

SQL has reordered the table in alphabetical order with respect to the names of the counties in the table. The output by default is in the ascending order from A to Z. Let's change the output otherwise.

SELECT * FROM Accounts

ORDER BY Country DESC;

Let's see the result.

Sr no.	AccountNumber	Name	Gender	Country
2	126545	Emily	Female	The United States
6	564578	Eric	Male	The United States
3	748525	Mary	Female	The United Kingdom
4	984578	Edwin	Male	The Netherlands
7	964578	Jimmy	Male	Switzerland
1	8596457	John	Male	Germany
5	895623	Ashwin	Male	Australia

The INSERT INTO Statement

This statement is very useful in big corporations where you have to add more and more data into the existing tables. You can add as much information in the existing tables as you like. See first how the table is in its original form.

Sr no.	AccountNumber	Name	Gender	Country
1	8596457	John	Male	Germany
2	126545	Emily	Female	The United States
3	748525	Mary	Female	The United Kingdom

Sr no.	AccountNumber	Name	Gender	Country
4	984578	Edwin	Male	The Netherlands
5	895623	Ashwin	Male	Australia
6	564578	Eric	Male	The United States
7	964578	Jimmy	Male	Switzerland

Let's see how to do that.

INSERT INTO Accounts (AccountNumber, Name, Gender, Country)

VALUES ('5485967', 'Katty', 'Female', 'Egypt');

Sr no.	AccountNumber	Name	Gender	Country
1	8596457	John	Male	Germany
2	126545	Emily	Female	United States
3	748525	Mary	Female	The United Kingdom
4	984578	Edwin	Male	The Netherlands
5	895623	Ashwin	Male	Australia
6	564578	Eric	Male	The United States
7	964578	Jimmy	Male	Switzerland

Sr no.	AccountNumber	Name	Gender	Country
8	5485967	Katty	Female	Egypt

You can see that the eighth record has been added to the end of the table. That's how you can insert as many records as you need. In addition, you also have the option to insert data into the columns of your choice. See how the table currently is stored in the database.

Sr no.	AccountNumber	Name	Gender	Country
1	8596457	John	Male	Germany
2	126545	Emily	Female	The United States
3	748525	Mary	Female	The United Kingdom
4	984578	Edwin	Male	The Netherlands
5	895623	Ashwin	Male	Australia
6	564578	Eric	Male	The United States
7	964578	Jimmy	Male	Switzerland

INSERT INTO Accounts (AccountNumber, Name, Country)

VALUES ('5485967', 'Katty', 'Egypt');

Sr no.	AccountNumber	Name	Gender	Country
1	8596457	John	Male	Germany
2	126545	Emily	Female	United States
3	748525	Mary	Female	The United Kingdom
4	984578	Edwin	Male	The Netherlands
5	895623	Ashwin	Male	Australia
6	564578	Eric	Male	The United States
7	964578	Jimmy	Male	Switzerland
8	5485967	Katty	Null	Egypt

SQL UPDATE Statement

This statement is largely used to modify the data which is already in the tables. This statement is paired up with the WHERE class that makes the decision which record you want to update. Here is our current table.

Sr no.	AccountNumber	Name	Gender	Country
1	8596457	John	Male	Germany
2	126545	Emily	Female	The United States

Sr no.	AccountNumber	Name	Gender	Country
3	748525	Mary	Female	The United Kingdom
4	984578	Edwin	Male	The Netherlands
5	895623	Ashwin	Male	Australia
6	564578	Eric	Male	The United States
7	964578	Jimmy	Male	Switzerland

UPDATE Accounts

SET Name = 'Jasmine'

WHERE AccountNumber = 5485967;

Sr no.	AccountNumber	Name	Gender	Country
1	8596457	John	Male	Germany
2	126545	Emily	Female	United States
3	748525	Mary	Female	The United Kingdom
4	984578	Edwin	Male	The Netherlands
5	895623	Ashwin	Male	Australia
6	564578	Eric	Male	The United States

Sr no.	AccountNumber	Name	Gender	Country
7	964578	Jimmy	Male	Switzerland
8	5485967	Jasmine	Null	Egypt

In the above example, I have updated a single record. You can update multiple records in the table by the following method. The current table is as below. After that, we will move on to the changes that the SQL statement will bring.

Sr no.	AccountNumber	Name	Gender	Country
1	8596457	John	Male	Germany
2	126545	Emily	Female	The United States
3	748525	Mary	Female	The United Kingdom
4	984578	Edwin	Male	The Netherlands
5	895623	Ashwin	Male	Australia
6	564578	Eric	Male	The United States
7	964578	Jimmy	Male	Switzerland

Now let's try the statement on the SQL server.

UPDATE Accounts

SET Name = 'Kitty', Country = 'Macedonia'

WHERE SrNo = 3;

Let's see the result.

Sr no.	AccountNumber	Name	Gender	Country
1	8596457	John	Male	Germany
2	126545	Emily	Female	United States
3	748525	Kitty	Female	Macedonia
4	984578	Edwin	Male	The Netherlands
5	895623	Ashwin	Male	Australia
6	564578	Eric	Male	The United States
7	964578	Jimmy	Male	Switzerland
8	5485967	Jasmine	Null	Egypt

The command has successfully updated two records in the Sr No. 3. That becomes very helpful for bankers who have to deal with clients who keep multiple accounts. They can update their account numbers without overhauling the entire table or entering complete information.

Let's see if you fail to use the WHERE clause. See first the current form of the table.

Sr no.	AccountNumber	Name	Gender	Country
1	8596457	John	Male	Germany

Sr no.	AccountNumber	Name	Gender	Country
2	126545	Emily	Female	The United States
3	748525	Mary	Female	The United Kingdom
4	984578	Edwin	Male	The Netherlands
5	895623	Ashwin	Male	Australia
6	564578	Eric	Male	The United States
7	964578	Jimmy	Male	Switzerland

Now run the statement in SQL.

UPDATE Accounts

SET Name = 'Kitty', Country = 'Macedonia'

Here is the result.

Sr no.	AccountNumber	Name	Gender	Country
1	8596457	Kitty	Male	Macedonia
2	126545	Kitty	Female	Macedonia
3	748525	Kitty	Female	Macedonia
4	984578	Kitty	Male	Macedonia
5	895623	Kitty	Male	Macedonia
6	564578	Kitty	Male	Macedonia
7	964578	Kitty	Male	Macedonia
8	5485967	Kitty	Null	Macedonia

A slight mistake can completely disrupt the system. It is important that you use the WHERE clause correctly (SQL Update Statement, n.d).

Chapter 15:
Introduction of Python

The first thing you need to do while learning Python is install it on your computer. Coupled with that is the installation of a text editor that is either python-specific or is python-supported. The text editor's job is to identify the Python code. They add colors to the different sections of your code as you write, which makes it readable and understandable.

If you are a Linux user, you will find it easier and fun to learn. Let's write the first script in the shell window of Python.

>>> print("Angels are falling from the heavens.")

Angels are falling from the heavens.

>>>

The above snippet of code is a complete program. This can be one of the smallest programs on Python, but it works as well as the largest programs. And if it runs well, bigger programs will run as well too.

Python is considered as a cross-platform programming language because it runs on every major operating system. It means that any kind of Python program that you write runs on any computer if you install Python on it. The way of installation may differ across different systems, but the function remains the same. The ultimate basic part of learning Python is to set up the Python first on your system and making it operational.

If you are a Linux user, you will get Python installed on your computer system already. Almost all Linux systems have conditions all set up for programming. For Windows users, there is an easy way to run Python. You need to download and install Python on your computer system. The next step is to install a text editor. You can edit your text on the editor and then run it on the Python shell.

When I ran the simple program, "Angels are falling from the heavens", the output came out pretty fast. Although it appears simple, the Python shell did lots of work in the background. As with all the other languages, Python too has variables which you can use as the following.

outcome = "Angels are falling from the heavens."

print(outcome)

When you run the code, you will receive the same output as you had received previously. The screen will display the following line:

Angels are falling from the heavens.

I added a variable named outcome to the code and assigned it the same value as I previously had printed. Variables carry values that you assign them. This feature allows you to inject important data into a specific variable. Let's learn to add more value to the variable outcome.

```
outcome = "Angels are falling from the heavens."
print(outcome)
outcome = "They seem to be on fire."
print(outcome)
```

The result will be something as the following:

Angels are falling from the heavens.

They seem to be on fire.

An important thing to note that you should add a single blank line between the two values of the variable to make it function properly. There are rules to follow when it comes to variables. If you don't follow them, your code will run an error.

There are some rules to follow when you are using variables in Python programming. Failing which can result in errors when you run the program. It is important that the variable you use contain numbers, underscores, and letters. In addition, they must not start with the number. Also, you cannot include spaces in the names. Instead, you can use underscores to separate different names in the variable. It is important that you don't use Python keywords as variables. Also, the variables you use should be self-explanatory. They can describe the purpose for which you are using them (Mathess, 2016).

Python is sensitive about spellings in the code. I'll misspell the variable in the code to see what happens as the result.

```
>>> print(outcome)
```

Angels are falling from the heavens.

>>> print(otcome)

Traceback (most recent call last):

  File "<pyshell#6>", line 1, in <module>

    print(otcome)

NameError: name 'otcome' is not defined

>>>

If you see the above reply in the Python shell, it means you have misspelled the name of the variable. The shell also tells us which variable is misspelled. By misspelling, it doesn't mean that the code has to follow the standard English spelling and grammar rules. Instead it should follow the spelling that you have written while creating a variable. Let's demonstrate this.

>>> otcome = "Angels are falling from the heavens."

>>> print(otcome)

Angels are falling from the heavens.

>>>

Strings

As with all the other programming languages, there are different data types in Python. One of them is the string in which you can store multiple characters in the form of a string. You can add single or double quotation marks to enclose characters in a string. This feature permits you to include even apostrophes in your strings. You can use strings for some pretty basic and simple tasks like printing different names in lowercases and uppercase. I'll create a variable first.

car = "mercedez benz"

>>> print(car.title())

Mercedez Benz

>>>

Note: This is a short program. If you write this program in the text editor, you can save it as car.py. and run it anytime. The "py" extension denotes that you are saving it as a python file. I stored the string in a variable. You might be wondering why are the parenthesis empty. Let me explain. I have employed a method to transform the first letters of the string into uppercase when it is printed on the shell screen. The title method doesn't require any additional information that's why the parenthesis is empty. There are other methods that require additional information which you can place inside the parenthesis.

The title method transforms the first letter of every word into uppercase. Let's try something exciting by using some other methods in the strings. We'll go with the same variable that we have created earlier on. For your ease, let's repeat the drill. I'll create the program in the Python shell to make it easy to grasp for you.

>>> car = "mercedez benz"

>>> print(car.upper())

MERCEDEZ BENZ

```
>>> print(car.lower())
mercedez benz
>>>
```

You can use these methods to store the information left by your users and then print it in future in the form it makes most sense.

You can also combine different strings. You might have come across different online services that require you to put your first name and last name in separate boxes. In addition, there also is no restriction in place for using uppercase or lowercase. If you are at the backend of the user service, you can store two different strings in different variables to be able to easily identify them and later on combine them when needed.

Let's see how to get the information in two strings and then combine it when it is required.

```
>>> car_name = "mercedez benz"
>>> make = "2018"
>>> details = car_name + " " + make
>>> print(details)
mercedez benz 2018
```

It is easy to understand the combination formula as it uses a simple mathematical (+) sign to pair up different strings into a single variable.

This method of combining different strings into a

single one is dubbed as concatenation. In addition to combining multiple strings into one, this method can also be used to draft messages for a single variable.

When you enter the tab or the spacebar or enter, it prints a whitespace in the world of coding. Usually whitespaces are used to make the code reader-friendly. The procedure of adding whitespaces to your code words is simple.

```
>>> print("meredez benz")
```

meredez benz

```
>>> print("\mercedez benz")
```

        mercedez benz

```
>>>
```

Another whitespace to be used is the new line feature.

```
>>>                                    print("Car
Models:\n\tAudi\n\tMercedez\n\tFerrari\n\tBentle
y\n\tBMW")
```

Car Models:

        Audi

        Mercedez

        Ferrari

        Bentley

        BMW

It is pertinent to understand here that Python is very sensitive to whitespaces. You cannot add whitespace without proper explanation.

Many programmers, who are at the beginning of their career, get frustrated due to repeated syntax errors while they are producing strings. This can happen due to some very basic mistakes while you are writing a code. If you don't use the single and double quotation marks in the way they are meant to be used, you will get syntax error as a result. Using apostrophes in a string can be tricky if you are enclosing it within the single quotes. The error emerges out of the fact that python read everything between the first single quote and the apostrophe as a separate string.

>>> carinfo = "Germany' s mercedez benz"

>>> print(carinfo)

Germany' s mercedez benz

The above is the correct use of the single and double quotation marks. Now I'll show you the wrong use.

carinfo = 'Germany' s mercedez benz'

SyntaxError: invalid syntax

You can create multiple files as practice. Try to run them on the shell and see their results. If any one of them runs into error, see the syntax to find out if there is any error in the composition. This might be frustrating as this kind of error is not specified in the result. You have to locate this manually in the code. Now that you know how to create strings, you will be able to compose messages, storing information in uppercase and lowercase, combining different strings into one and also using quotation marks in the right way.

More Data Types

Data in Python is also stored in the form of numbers. Python makes it easier for programmers to store and use data. Let's see how it treats the integers. I'll use python to perform simple mathematical functions like addition, multiplication, subtraction, and division.

>>> 45*23

1035

>>> 96+36

132

>>> 654-96

558

>>> 555/5

111.0

Just open a shell window and try it out. You will get instant results from the shell window. Python also fully understands the order of the mathematical operations. I'll demonstrate it for your ease.

>>> 25*36+45

945

>>> 63*45*69+89-1000+2000/300

194710.66666666666

You don't have to guide it on what to do first. It reads the values you enter in the shell and does the calculations in the blink of an eye. If you put all the mathematical symbols in the single line without inserting parentheses, it will perform standard operations. But you can guide the shell to do how you want it to do.

>>> 25*25+25

650

>>> 25*(25+25)

1250

Parenthesis can help you guide the shell while doing some complex multiplications. Divisions in python can be tricky as the result is likely to be in decimals. The numbers in decimals are called float in Python. In Java, it has the same name. Decimals can be tricky to handle; that's why they should be properly used and stored.

>>> 25.60+50.23+900.25

976.08

>>> 23*55

1265

>>> 23*69/39

40.69230769230769

Decoding the Lists and Dictionaries

We have now understood that strings are used to store pieces of text and integers. We can store many pieces of information in a multiple strings and get the desired outcome by combining them. That's an easy way to store information on a small scale. For a bigger scale, we can use lists to store millions of items. You can be able to pack up many pieces of information inside a list.

Just like we formed lists in HTML, a list in Python contains pieces of information ordered in a specific form. A list may contain names and numbers. In addition, python doesn't distinguish among different pieces of information. For example, it doesn't differentiate between names of presidents of the United States and parts of computer. You can pack both in a single list.

How Can I Identify a List?

In python, the square brackets [] denotes a list. You can enter more than one elements in a list by inserting a comma after each. Let's create one.

>>> cars = ['audi', 'ferrari', 'bentley', 'mercedez benz', 'bmw']

>>> print(cars)

['audi', 'ferrari', 'bentley', 'mercedez benz', 'bmw']

You can pretty easily access the individual items in the list.

>>> print(cars[4])

bmw

>>> print(cars[0])

audi

```
>>> print(cars[2])

Bentley

>>> print(cars[3])

mercedez benz

>>> print(cars[1])

ferrari
```

You can offer your users to find out each individual item in a particular list of items. They can access a single item from the list and view the contents. The printed item will not be enclosed inside brackets. If you have a list formed by python, you can use the method of concatenation to create a new outcome by picking up an item from the list and integrating in the code of your outcome. Let's try to create your customized outcome with two items from the list.

```
outcome = "My garage is packed with a " +
cars[2].title() + "."
```

My garage is packed with a Bentley.

You can also modify elements of a list by injecting and removing different elements. For example, you are creating a game by using Python. For this purpose, you store different players in one list, all the guns the players can use in another list, and the props that the player can pick up from the street in the third list. When one player uses a gun or a prop, it is removed from the list of elements. This suggests that lists are pretty dynamic in Python. Let's see how can you modify a list of elements. You can use the same syntax that you use to create or access an item from the list. After you have accessed a particular item that you want to modify, you can fill in the new value.

>>> cars = ['audi', 'ferrari', 'bentley', 'mercedez benz', 'bmw']

>>> print(cars)

['audi', 'ferrari', 'bentley', 'mercedez benz', 'bmw']

>>> cars[2] = 'lamborghini'

>>> print(cars)

['audi', 'ferrari', 'lamborghini', 'mercedez benz', 'bmw']

You can see that the third item from the list has been modified with a new value. We don't have to prepare a new list if we have to modify a couple of values in it.

Note: It is important to note that the list is numbered from zero onwards. It means zero if for the first item and one is for the second item on the list.

You can also add new elements to the existing list. I will use the append feature of python language to add something to the current list. We have modified the list earlier on with the new car model named lamborghini. I will use the same car model for addition in the list instead of mere modification because I want the other car model to remain in its place.

cars = ['audi', 'ferrari', 'bentley', 'mercedez benz', 'bmw']

>>> print(cars)

['audi', 'ferrari', 'bentley', 'mercedez benz', 'bmw']

>>> cars.append('lamborghini')

>>> print(cars)

['audi', 'ferrari', 'bentley', 'mercedez benz', 'bmw', 'lamborghini']

We have successfully added the car model lamborghini in the list. All the other items of the list stand intact. Some people find it too taxing to do thing in a go. They can really benefit from the appending feature as they can easily add items to the list using this feature even if the list is empty in the start. You can keep your users' data streamlined with the help of this feature. Just create a new list for each user and keep adding new data into it as you receive it along the way.

When you append a list, you are adding items to the end of it. You can also add items in the middle of in the start or wherever you like by the insert feature in python.

cars = ['audi', 'ferrari', 'bentley', 'mercedez benz', 'bmw']

>>> cars.insert(2, 'super car')

>>> print(cars)

['audi', 'ferrari', 'super car', 'bentley', 'mercedez benz', 'bmw']

We have successfully added a new item in the middle of the list. Now the thing is that you also can delete the items from a particular list if you like. It happens more often when you want to get rid of some data from a particular list, owing to its irrelevance or lack of need. For example, you have a list of guns that you have provided for the players. Whenever he has picked one, you need to remove it from the list to keep the game dynamic. For the purpose you need to use the del statement. Let's apply this code on the list of cars that we already have modified and updated with the insert feature of python.

```
>>> cars = ['audi', 'ferrari', 'bentley', 'mercedez benz', 'bmw']
>>> del cars[1]
>>> print(cars)
['audi', 'bentley', 'mercedez benz', 'bmw']
```

If we replace 1 with 0, 2, or 3, we can delete any item, even the entire list one by one. If the player has exhausted the bag of guns, we can delete them one by one so that the bag appears empty when the player approached it next time. Once you have deleted an item, you cannot access it.

But if you need a deleted item to work in future? For example, you have to prepare another list of guns that a player has used in order to show him what has been utilized. Here you can use the pop method which allows to work on a list items after you have removed them from the real list.

```
cars = ['audi', 'ferrari', 'bentley', 'mercedez benz', 'bmw']
>>> print(cars)
```

['audi', 'ferrari', 'bentley', 'mercedez benz', 'bmw']

>>> popped_cars = cars.pop()

>>> print(cars)

['audi', 'ferrari', 'bentley', 'mercedez benz']

>>> print(popped_cars)

bmw

The item at the end of list has been popped out but even after removal, you can print it on the shell and work on it. You can literally pop out an item from the list. You keep applying this feature and one item will be popped out each time until nothing remains in the list.

>>> popped_cars = cars.pop()

>>> print(cars)

['audi', 'ferrari', 'bentley']

>>> popped_cars = cars.pop()

>>> print(cars)

['audi', 'ferrari']

>>> popped_cars = cars.pop()

>>> print(cars)

['audi']

>>> popped_cars = cars.pop()

>>> print(cars)

[]

Now you can print any item from the list for working on it.

>>> cars = ['audi', 'ferrari', 'bentley', 'mercedez benz', 'bmw']

>>> first_owned = cars.pop(2)

>>> print(cars)

['audi', 'ferrari', 'mercedez benz', 'bmw']

I have successfully removed the third item from the list. This method can add more dynamics to the program, web application or game you are building with python.

How to Loop Through the List You Have Created?

Now we know that we can add or remove or modify an item in a list. If you want to run the same action through the entire list, you need to work with the loops. By using this feature, you can add more dynamics to your programs and games. For example, every item on the screen can work simultaneously by following the same action at the same time after you set a loop for it.

We will use the for loop for involving each item in the list in some sort of action. Let's see the same list of cars that we have been using since the start of the chapter. We can print each item on the list individually with the print command or we can put the list in the for loop to sit aside and see how the loop runs each item on the list efficiently and fast.

```
>>> cars = ['audi', 'ferrari', 'bentley', 'mercedez benz',
'bmw']
>>> for car in cars:
        print(car)
```

audi

ferrari

bentley

mercedez benz

bmw

At first we have defined the list then we have defined the for loop and also told the shell to pick up each name from the list and print it on the screen. The loop will run through each item that you have on the list and print likewise print each item. This is the very basis of automation as by this method you can direct a computer or a web application to automatically execute a certain task. In the loop that I have created for you, it is easy to understand that Python reads the loop first, understands the action that is required then moves on to read each item on the list and act as per directions. I directed it to print each item on the list which it did.

This loop can be created for a list of 10,000 items. It will stop only after running through the last item. This is amazing! You can save lots of time and energy with this kind of automation feature. Let's do something exciting with the loops. We will create a list of sold cars for the users to see on the website. Whatever item is added to the list will be displayed as sold.

```
>>> cars = ['audi', 'ferrari', 'bentley', 'mercedez benz', 'bmw']
>>> for car in cars:
        print(car.title() + ", has been sold!")
```

Audi, has been sold!

Ferrari, has been sold!

Bentley, has been sold!

Mercedez Benz, has been sold!

Bmw, has been sold!

Isn't it amazing? You can perform this action on each item of the list in a matter of seconds. You can combine different actions in a single loop to make it more fun. For example, you want to add a line to each car that the stock will be refilled on the next Monday. In this way your users will have more information available for each item and they won't have to concert the helpline, saving you money which would otherwise have been spent on a customer representative. Let's add more lines of code to the existing loop.

```
>>> cars = ['audi', 'ferrari', 'bentley', 'mercedez benz', 'bmw']
>>> for car in cars:
        print(car.title() + ", has been sold and the
```

stock is empty!")

       print("Don't worry the stock will be refreshed on the next Monday")

Audi, has been sold and the stock is empty!

Don't worry the stock will be refreshed on the next Monday

Ferrari, has been sold and the stock is empty!

Don't worry the stock will be refreshed on the next Monday

Bentley, has been sold and the stock is empty!

Don't worry the stock will be refreshed on the next Monday

Mercedez Benz, has been sold and the stock is empty!

Don't worry the stock will be refreshed on the next Monday

Bmw, has been sold and the stock is empty!

Don't worry the stock will be refreshed on the next Monday

In this way you can use multiple code lines to run through the loop.

Chapter 16:
Moving Further into the World of Python

Functions are considered as blocks of code that are designed to perform a particular job. A function only runs when you call it in the midst of the code. You need to define the function first in order to call it and run it successfully. Function makes it easy for you to do repeat tasks again and again. Whenever you need to do the same task, you just call the designated function. You will get the job done fast and efficiently in a fraction of the time you would have consumed had you rewritten the entire function.

Once you master the art of functions, you will be able to write your programs in a timely and efficient manner. Every function contains a set of information that you pass on to it. It stores the information and executes the program when you call it later on as needed. Let's see how you can write them and execute them when you need them during drafting a code.

The Python Functions

Creation of function is dubbed as defining the function in the world of programming. I will define my first function.

```
>>> def paradise_lost():

    """Display the theme of the book."""

    print("Angels are falling from the heavens.")


>>> paradise_lost()
```

Angels are falling from the heavens.

This can be one of the simplest structures among functions. Let us dissect the code to understand it by heart.

- The *def* in the function is the keyword which informs Python that a function is ready to be defined. You can say that *def* means defined. This keyword helps Python to know what will be the name of your function. In more complex functions, the parenthesis after the name is filled with the information that Python demands to do its job. In simple functions like the abovementioned, the parenthesis stays empty. The definition line ends up in a colon (;).
- The indented lines after the keyword def are termed as the body of the function. The second line that is enclosed inside three double quotation marks is termed as the docstring. It describes what a function does. Python sees it and documents it as an explanation for what the function is intended for.
- The third line contains the code which the function has to perform upon calling by a user. In this case the function has to print the line: Angels are falling from the heavens.

- The last task is to call the function, which can be done simply by writing the name of the function. There is parenthesis at the end of the name of the function that may contain additional information if needed. As our function is a simple one, we don't have to put additional information inside the parenthesis.

Modifying the Function

A good thing about functions is that we can modify them easily. Passing on relevant information to an existing function can be done by writing a simple code.

def paradise_lost(username):

"""Angels are falling from the heavens."""

print("Hello. " + username.title() + "!")

paradise_lost('Satan is watching on the earth')

When you call the function, it will show the existing plus the passed on value. Whatever we put in the single quotation marks in the last line of the function is dubbed as arguments while username in the parenthesis is dubbed as a parameter.

def paradise_lost(sname):

  print(sname + " Smith")

paradise_lost("John")

paradise_lost("Tobby")

paradise_lost("Jacob")

paradise_lost("Tutsy")

The result is as below:

John Smith

Tobby Smith

Jacob Smith

Tutsy Smith

I used the parameter (sname) then kept passing on values through the parameter to the real function. That's how you can add as many values to the function as you want to (Python Functions, n.d).

Let's see another example.

def paradise_lost(sname):

  print(sname + " Satan is watching them fall on in the lake of fire")

paradise_lost("Angels are falling from the heavens.")

paradise_lost("Angles are banished from the heavens.")

paradise_lost("Once they were the rulers of heavens.")

paradise_lost("Angels have been punished.")

The result is as below:

Angels are falling from the heavens. Satan is watching them fall on in the lake of fire

Angles are banished from the heavens. Satan is watching them fall on in the lake of fire

Once they were the rulers of heavens. Satan is watching them fall on in the lake of fire

Angels have been punished. Satan is watching them fall on in the lake of fire

Let's pass on to the function new values from a different way. This time, I will add the function parameter to the end of each argument that I allot to the function.

```python
def paradise_lost(place = "heavens"):
  print("Angels are living in the " + place)
```

```python
paradise_lost("Hell.")
```

```python
paradise_lost("Earth.")
```

```python
paradise_lost()
```

```python
paradise_lost("Mountain.")
```

```python
paradise_lost("lake of fire where they are destined to live for eternity. From there they will execute their evil operations as the slaves of Satan")
```

Let's see the result in the shell.

Angels are living in the Hell.

Angels are living in the Earth.

Angels are living in the heavens

Angels are living in the Mountain.

Angels are living in the lake of fire where they are destined to live for eternity. From there they will execute their evil operations as the slaves of Satan

You can do complex arithmetic operations with the help of the return function. It will do the math and return the value on the shell screen. Let's try to do some. Please remember you can copy this code and paste it in the Python shell to get result in order to practice how this function works. You can change the mathematical values to customize the code and learn it by heart.

```python
def paradise_lost(y):
  return 50 + y *1000

print(paradise_lost(23))

print(paradise_lost(55))

print(paradise_lost(95))

print(paradise_lost(111))
```

The result on the Python shell will be as below:

23050

55050

95050

111050

Classes and Objects

Nowadays, programmers prefer object-oriented programming for building software. Classes in python and any other object-oriented programming are used to build real life objects. You can assign them certain attributes which the object enjoys in the real world. A class may contain a full string of characteristics that reflect the person's behavior. You can edit the traits that object can have or should have according to your opinion. You are the creator here so you can do whatever you like. You can create real-life situations through object-oriented programming and classes play a great role in materializing that.

The process of creation of objects is named as instantiation, which suggests you will be working with instances of a particular class. Let's take a look at the steps involved in the process:

- You will have to write a class.
- You will create instances.
- You will have to provide data for storing in the instances you have created earlier on.
- You will have to define the actions that you need your instances to take.
- You will have to write more classes that would execute the existing classes.
- After that you will have to store your classes inside modules and then import those classes to certain program files in which you want them

Let's try it on.

```
class ParadiseLost:

 y = 100


p1 = ParadiseLost()

print(p1.y)
```

I did two things in the above-mentioned code. First thing was to create a class named as ParadiseLost. The second thing I did was to create an object titled as p1.

The __inti__() method is one of the vital elements in classes and objects section of Python. The above is a function, but as it is used as a part of a class, it is dubbed as a method. This method is run by Python when we create a new instance.

```
class Car:

 def __init__(self, name, model):

        self.name = name

        self.model = model


p1 = Car("BMW", 2019)


print(p1.name)

print(p1.model)
```

See the result:

BMW

2019

Now, let's insert a function inside the class.

```
class Car:
  def __init__(obj, name, model):
      obj.name = name
      obj.model = model
  def myfunc(obj):
    print("Hello I am " + obj.name)
p1 = Car("BMW", 2019)
p1.myfunc()
```

Let's see the result on the screen.

Hello I am BMW.

In the above code, we have assigned a function to the object BMW. The car tells her name to the audience. I have replaced the self parameter with obj just to show that you can name it whatever you like. This is how classes are used to create objects in Python.

Creating a personalized class in Python

With the following class, we will be able to store a car's model name and year of production. This class will also give the car some additional animating abilities.

```
class Car():
        """This class will model an automated car."""
        def __init__(self, model, year):
```

"""It is time to initialize the name as well as age attributes."""

self.model = model

self.year = year

def sit(self):

"""This will keep the car in its place when you command it so."""

print(self.name.title() + " is now sitting in its place.")

def roll_over(self):

"""This option will simulate spinning over in response to a command."""

print(self.name.title() + " spinning over!")

(Mathess, 2016)

Tuples in Python

A tuple in Python is a collection of items that you just cannot change. You have to write tuples enclosed in round brackets or parenthesis as they are commonly called.

mytuple = ("BMW", "Buggati", "Mercedez")

print(mytuple)

The list goes on as the following:

"BMW", "Buggati", "Mercedez"

You can access whichever item you want from the

tuple. An interesting thing about tuples is that you can access them easily from the starting as well as the ending points.

mytuple = ("BMW", "Buggati", "Mercedez")

print(mytuple)

print(mytuple[0])

print(mytuple[1])

print(mytuple[2])

print(mytuple[-2])

print(mytuple[-1])

The result is as below:

('BMW', 'Buggati', 'Mercedez')

BMW

Buggati

Mercedez

Buggati

Mercedez

Buggati

Mercedez

As a general rule, tuples are unchangeable, but there is a way out of it. You can convert the tuple into a list, then change the list and after that convert it once again into a tuple. Let's do that.

mytuple = ("BMW", "Buggati", "Mercedez", "Suzuki Liana", "Prius", "Grande")

x = ("BMW", "Buggati", "Mercedez", "Suzuki Liana", "Prius", "Grande")

y = list(x)

y[2] = "Mehran"

x = tuple(y)

print(x)

It will result in the following:

('BMW', 'Buggati', 'Mercedez', 'Suzuki Liana', 'Prius', 'Grande')

Managing Strings in Python

Text is considered as the most-common and the most-reliable and user-friendly type of data in any programming language. Strings allow us flexibility to edit the data which has already been stored in different variables. You can extract a piece of data, add into the existing one, remove a piece of data from the storage, and add or remove spacing in the data. You can also change the case of a certain sentence, word or phrase by converting it into uppercase or lowercase. In addition to doing these wonders, you can copy a piece of text on the clipboard and paste elsewhere. This section sheds light on the working of strings and how can you manage the data through manipulating strings. With the help of Python, you can also automate text formatting.

The string literals

Allocating pieces of texts to a string is a simple task. You can easily do that in the shell by adding single quotation marks at the start and the end. You need to understand that Python is sensitive about the use of quotation marks. Let's see.

>>> mystring = 'My dad'll bring my car'

SyntaxError: invalid syntax

>>> mystring = "My dad'll bring my car"

>>> print(mystring)

My dad'll bring my car

If you misuse the quotation marks, it will interpret it in the wrong way and display erroneous results. And this is the last thing you want. The double quotation marks in the start tells Python that there is an apostrophe in the string which is part of the string and not the Python code. Otherwise, it considers the apostrophe as the end of the string and gets confused by the real single quotation mark at the ultimate end of the string. You get a syntax error as a result.

The Escape Characters in Python

An escape character is used to insert characters into a string that would have been impossible to put in otherwise. The creators of Python took into consideration the possible glitches that could come across the way of programmers. An escape character can be remembered by considering it a way to escape problems while you are coding. We have seen that using an apostrophe in a code can lead to a syntax error if the entire string is enclosed in single quotation marks. You can escape from running this kind of syntax error by inserting an escape character into the string. See how to do that.

```
>>> mystring = 'My dad\'ll bring my car'
```

```
>>> print(mystring)
```

My dad'll bring my car

```
>>>
```

Python is created so as to read the backslash and understand that the following single quote is not a quote but an apostrophe. It reads it accordingly and ignores it as a single quotation mark. As a result, the code runs successfully without any kind of syntax error.

```
>>> mystring = "My dad'll bring my car. I will\t take you for a ride."
```

```
>>> print(mystring)
```

My dad'll bring my car. I will   take you for a ride.

The character \t is used to insert a tab in between the lines.

```
>>> mystring = "My dad'll bring my car. \nI will take you for a ride."
```

```
>>> print(mystring)
```

My dad'll bring my car.

I will take you for a ride.

The escape character \n is for starting a new line in a string. It is useful because some text cannot be written on the same line as the other text. With the help of this escape character, it becomes super easy to distinguish among different pieces of texts.

If you want the shell to ignore all escape characters in the text and simply print it out, you can use the raw string option.

```
>>> mystring = (r"My dad'll bring my car. \nI will take you for a ride.")
>>> print(mystring)
```

My dad'll bring my car. \nI will take you for a ride.

```
>>>
```

Conclusion

Now that you have made it till the end, I would like you to push the replay button in your brain and think about what you have learnt about a certain programming language. Are you ready to delve further into the world of programming? Has it touched a chord in your heart? Is it exciting or completely boring? It is easy to tell. You have made it till the end on the back the excitement coding has brought to you. You are ready to move on.

Why is Learning Computer Programming Highly Beneficial for You?

Computer programming is a highly paid and sought-after profession in the world. You can find a lucrative career in a matter of a few years if only you train yourself well for taking up big challenges and finding solutions to things that bother the world. You can be highly successful if only you are comfortable with working on a dark screen and if you can enclose yourself in a dim-lit room. Computer programmers are well-off because they are paid great. And why not? You are making computers their slaves who would act on whatever they are ordered. This sort of immense customization of computers has brought about a revolution in the world of corporate business. Each new programming language brings something new to offer while keeping the basics from the other languages. This is how learning new things is easier.

Computer programming is considered as one of the top career options because it offers professionals the freedom to create new things all the time. Once you have learned enough, you are able to write programs, automate different tasks, and make your computer do things fast and efficiently. You can either serve as an in-house employee where you can rule the floor by solving intricate problems or you can do it as a freelancer in return for a hefty paycheck. Freelancing is one of the greatest advantages of learning programming because you have the freedom to work for different companies and get paid per project. All you have to do is turn on your computer and create your client a website, a web application, or software for the cash counter of their superstore.

This is a dynamically evolving field. When you have learned four to five programming languages, you are in a good position to take up any new language that enters the market. This helps you stay up to date with the latest developments in the cyber world, so that you can keep up with the changes and shift your preferences and orientations accordingly. You will never be out of work if you learn it by heart and also stay up to date with the latest skills.

Once you have mastered computer programming languages, you will be hard to beat. Corporations are always looking out for experienced and qualified programmers to take up their problems with computers, databases, and websites. This opens up tons of opportunities for computer programmers. You can not only learn a lot along the way, but you also can make millions of dollars.

References

12 Benefits of SQL (Structured Query Language). Retrieved from:https://www.systematix.co.uk/tips-tricks/12-benefits-of-sql-structured-query-language

Advantages of HTML. Retrieved from: https://www.educba.com/advantages-of-html/

C++ Getting Started. Retrieved from:https://www.w3schools.com/cpp/cpp_getstarted.asp

Duckett, John. (2011). HTML & CSS [PDF File].

Hanson, Chris. (2018). 6 Reasons You Need Dynamic Content. Retrieved from: https://www.sundoginteractive.com/blog/6-reasons-you-need-dynamic-content

Introduction to SQL. Retrieved from: https://www.w3schools.com/sql/sql_intro.asp

Java Data Types. Retrieved from: https://www.w3schools.com/java/java_data_types.asp

Java Arrays. Retrieved from: https://www.w3schools.com/java/java_arrays.asp

Matthes, Eric. (2016). PYTHON CRASH COURSE [PDF File].

Rongala, Arvind, (2015). Benefits of Python over Other Programming Languages. Retrieved from:https://www.invensis.net/blog/it/benefits-of-python-over-other-programming-languages/

SQL Operators. Retrieved from:
https://www.w3schools.com/sql/sql_operators.asp

SQL AND, OR and NOT Operators. Retrieved from:https://www.w3schools.com/sql/sql_and_or.asp

SQL Update Statement. Retrieved from:
https://www.javatpoint.com/dbms-sql-update

Strousturp, Bjarne. (2013). The C++ PROGRAMMING LANGUAGE [PDF File].

Varma, Kumar. (2018). What are the advantages of C++ Programming Language? Retrieved from:https://www.tutorialspoint.com/What-are-the-advantages-of-Cplusplus-Programming-Language